SALSA

SALSA
A Taste of Hispanic Culture

RAFAEL FALCÓN

in collaboration with Christine Yoder Falcón

PRAEGER

Westport, Connecticut
London

Library of Congress Cataloging-in-Publication Data

Falcón, Rafael.
　Salsa : a taste of Hispanic culture / Rafael Falcón, in collaboration with Christine Yoder Falcón.
　　p.　cm.
　Includes bibliographical references (p. –) and index.
　ISBN 0–275–96121–4 (alk. paper)
　1. Latin America—Social life and customs.　2. National characteristics, Latin American.　I. Falcón, Christine Yoder. II. Title.
　F1408.3.F34　1998
　980—dc21　　97–49285

British Library Cataloguing in Publication Data is available.

Library of Congress Catalog Card Number: 97–49285
ISBN: 0–275–96121–4

First published in 1998

Praeger Publishers, 88 Post Road West, Westport, CT 06881
An imprint of Greenwood Publishing Group, Inc.

Printed in the United States of America

The paper used in this book complies with the Permanent Paper Standard issued by the National Information Standards Organization (Z39.48–1984).

10　9　8　7　6　5　4　3　2　1

To Petronila Rosario de Meléndez, my maternal grandmother,
who nurtured and transmitted many beautiful Hispanic traditions.

Contents

Acknowledgments

The creation of this book could not have been accomplished without the assistance and contributions of many people. I would first like to thank my wife and collaborator, Christine, for her enthusiastic support for the project, for her thoroughness and patience in editing the manuscript, and for her many helpful and creative suggestions.

I would also like to acknowledge the work of several of my Goshen College colleagues who provided me with insightful comments, astute observations and constructive criticism: Judith Davis, Professor of French; Fernando Marroquín, Assistant Professor of Spanish; Ron Stutzman, Professor of Anthropology; and Ruth Krall, Professor of Religion.

In addition, I want to express my appreciation to Brooke Kandel, my student assistant, for her observations on the manuscript in general and specifically for her work with the glossary.

Finally, I acknowledge my gratitude to the Multicultural Affairs Office and the Academic Excellence Program of Goshen College for encouraging me to undertake this project through their provision of grants and for their unfaltering belief in its importance.

R.F.

Introduction

For cultural integration to occur, a knowledge of the habits, beliefs, patterns of behavior, and values of that culture is critically important. Indeed, understanding its expectations is as essential as knowing its language.

Involvement with this new environment offers an opportunity to appreciate how others cope with everyday life situations. The learner soon realizes that the cultural tendencies of the host group are not necessarily correct or incorrect, appropriate or inappropriate, better or worse; they are different. And ultimately adjustment to the culture's standards of behavior can become part of this learning adventure, most often without abandonment of one's personal value systems.

With such an understanding as its base, this book has been written to increase awareness of the idiosyncrasies of Hispanic culture; to inspire mutual respect and appreciate differences between cultures; to value the beauty of diversity; to show that understanding cultural nuances is as important as language in the interaction with and appreciation of an ethnic group; to comprehend the reasons for behavioral responses of a locale; and to become aware of the interconnectedness of this behavior with factors such as history, origin and weather.

This book has been written with a wide range of readers in mind. It has been created for those individuals who are minimally acquainted with the Hispanic culture and would like to become more informed; for high school and college students taking Spanish courses; for professionals teaching Hispanics in English as a Second Language (ESL) programs; for students who are planning to study abroad in Spanish-speaking countries; for high school and college Spanish teachers; and for anyone interested in helping to improve relationships among ethnic groups.

This challenging and enjoyable project is the result of personal motivation, encouraged at several levels. Having taught the Hispanic language, literature, and culture at the undergraduate level for over twenty years, I have become convinced of the need for a book that would capture aspects of the typical Hispanic culture. Since art, music, and literature have been more frequently researched and studied, my intent has been to focus on the daily routines and patterns of human interaction in society, cultural perspectives not usually addressed.

The many questions from my students, as well as from other people, also provided motivation. For example, curiosity about *quinceañeros, compadres, parrandas,* and *piropos* caused my list of topics to grow longer over the years.

Without a doubt, though, a very important contribution to my motivation has been my daily life as a Hispanic residing in a culture distinct from the one in which I spent my first twenty-eight years. In addition, my marriage to a North American has kept the reality of cultural ideas and analysis active on an almost constant basis.

This book has been grouped into twenty-six chapters relating to different themes. Each contains several related topics that collectively provide an understanding of cultural responses. In an attempt to furnish a context as real and personable as possible, each section begins with a personal story that illustrates one or more of the topics that follow it. These vignettes will hopefully transcend the pedagogical value of this collection, creating for the reader a sense of my culture as real as life. In addition, a glossary is included that contains those Spanish terms and phrases that are not translated as part of the text.

As one reads, it is essential to keep in mind that the Hispanic world covers a vast geographical area, and as such is a mosaic of ethnic, religious, and historical backgrounds. Because of this, a theme developed in this book may accurately describe the greater part of the Hispanic population, but may not necessarily represent every community or area. Indeed, therein lies the uniqueness, the texture, the flavor of each part, contributing collectively to the richness of the whole. This is the "salsa": a taste of Hispanic culture.

1

General Cultural Concepts

The dark-haired, blue-eyed man approached me as I stood on the front porch watching traffic and pedestrians pass by on a beautiful tropical afternoon. My father was home from work and wanted to engage me in a conversation about school events and issues. He moved two chairs from the living room out to the front porch and gestured for me to sit down. We chatted comfortably and amiably for a while. Then as we became more involved in our discussion, gestures became more animated and my father's chair inched closer to mine. His wide muscular hand was connecting with my small knee as he made significant statements. We were enjoying the moment: The warmth of the western sun slanted onto the porch; the conversation was spirited and interesting; we were emotionally close and the physical nearness felt comfortable. What did it matter that my knee had turned a light shade of red!

PERSONAL SPACE

The sense of ownership of an individual's personal space differs from one society to another. Within the Hispanic culture the area around one's person is relatively small, resulting in a comfortable physical nearness, which is especially noticeable between individuals as they converse. So it is, that even though unconscious, an interesting exchange of distance adjustments take place during a conversation between two individuals who come from distinct cultures or who have differing levels of personal space comfort. Let's imagine a conversation between José, a Costa Rican university graduate, and Ed, an exchange student from Ohio, with José feeling very much at ease standing quite close to a conversation partner while Ed needs distance. As the participants become more involved in their conversation, unconsciously, Ed feels he is standing too close to José, so he takes a slight step backward, thus feeling more comfortable. Without a second thought or conscious awareness, José feels a need to recuperate the conversational distance that has been lost, so he steps toward Ed. Though neither may be aware of this action, which may be repeated throughout the conversation, both are attempting to adjust to a comfortable personal space zone.

It is likely that José's conversation with Ed will also illustrate another typical characteristic of his culture: the use of gesture and touch while conversing. As Ed and José become more and more involved in the topic, José may repeatedly, although momentarily, touch Ed on the shoulder or on the arm or, if they are sitting down, the knee. Ed does not need to feel uncomfortable about this since this is a natural Hispanic way.

THE CONCEPT OF TIME

The concept of time is intrinsic to a culture, both affecting the society's behavioral patterns and being shaped by those same factors. In some cultures, time is viewed as a set structure that is measured in exact quantities, taking on the characteristics of money that is a personal possession needing to be used correctly, and that is saved, spent, or wasted. In others, time is perceived as a flexible framework, enabling the manipulation and enjoyment of the present moment.

It is this latter concept of time that is reflected in the living and working patterns within most Hispanic communities. Here the individual receives more respect than the schedule. Feeling little need to plan extensively beyond today, extended members of family, neighbors, and friends drop in to visit without calling ahead. A delay of fifteen to thirty minutes to a planned function is considered normal and is, in fact, expected. With fruits and vegetables produced year-round in most areas, the urgency to store harvest produce against scarcity in the future is not relevant. Though persons will make plans within their individual lives, the general cultural milieu concentrates on the relationships and events of the present and life is taken in stride. In this Spanish-language culture, even the clock "walks" (*el reloj anda*), while in English it "runs"!

Nevertheless, the economic structure of a given area affects the concept of time differently from one community to another within this same society. A setting largely dependent upon industry demands set hours and an emphasis upon punctuality, while farming in a rural mountainous area flows with the rising and setting of the sun. Some heavily industrialized regions of the Hispanic world exemplify this, with more stringent work expectations and regimented life style evident. In these areas public functions such as movie theaters, theatrical performances and larger businesses tend to run according to schedule, while nearby in *el campo*, the rural life is more *tranquila* and time moves at different pace.

TOUCH AND EMOTIONS

Hispanics are generally people *del corazón*, of the heart. More important than the rational to this culture is the emotional; feelings over logic. Integral to the cultural reality is the heart, integrating all communication and fact. Logic must be spoken with emotional expression and physical gesticulation in order to be heard.

Touch and warm positive feelings are easily expressed and embraces and hugs among friends are common. In fact, on occasions like birthdays, Christmas or New Year's Eve parties the act of embracing is standard as part of the festive spirit. Equally, in times of pain or mourning, support and solidarity are expressed with an embrace.

Even within the same gender, physical contact is culturally accepted. Women often walk arm in arm, especially a mother and daughter, or good friends. It is also very common for men to embrace each other or for a young man to put his arm or hand around the shoulder of a male friend as they walk along and talk. This is especially evidenced when friends have not seen each other for quite some time or when farewells with an anticipated long separation are said.

A kiss is also an expression of the heart. For a man and a woman to greet each other with a kiss on the cheek is a symbol of friendship and does not suggest romantic intention. On the other hand, a kiss on the lips is reserved for lovers, so even within the family setting, children and parents never kiss on the lips. There is also reserve in kissing in public. Spouses, for example, when saying good-bye to each other in public generally kiss on the cheek.

TACT AND DIPLOMACY

In the Hispanic culture tact and diplomacy are very much valued. The ultimate goal in the social setting is to provide an enjoyable and positive interaction among those involved. Thus, it is not uncommon for an individual to appear to agree with another on issues in a conversation, when in reality he/she does not. This is seen as a way of reducing conflict and promoting harmony and rapport. Thus, it is wise not to read too much into an expression of agreement.

Statements such as *"Quiero que comamos juntos algún día"* ("Let's have dinner together sometime") or *"Te voy a invitar a casa"* ("I'm going to invite you to my home") are tactful ways to express appreciation for the given friendship or relationship. They may or may not be specific invitations so they should be taken literally only when the person making the statement offers specific details about the activity or invitation.

PRIDE AND DIGNITY

Pride and dignity are also qualities that are very much valued. Considered completely apart from worldly or material possessions, these qualities are seen as emerging from that which is internal and inherent in each person. This concept of personal worth permits a more relaxed attitude toward societal rank: success is defined by how one conducts oneself within the social framework rather than upon one's position. One's role is held with pride and an attempt is made to live it with dignity.

Strongly connected with these culturally valued qualities comes an equally esteemed sense of worth placed on outward appearances. No matter how sparse the income, the intent is to dress as cleanly and neatly as possible regardless of the event—to go to the store or an important function. Even if this involves sacrifice, an effort is made to conform to the image the individual feels is expected of self by others.

HONOR

The concept of honor originated from Arabic influence and is still alive today in the Hispanic world. An individual's honor is based upon what others are supposedly thinking about one and one's family.

Historically, if one's honor became *manchado* (stained) through some verbal insult, sex scandal, physical aggression or such, the response was to "wash it" with blood. So it was that an arranged duel would be the chosen method to atone for an individual's lost honor. Unfortunately, even today in some places, that ancient custom of duels continues with the use of guns, knives or machetes in attempts to regain honor perceived to have been lost.

OLDER AGE

Unlike some cultures where value is placed on youthfulness or genius, age is esteemed in this society, with veneration shown toward the more elderly. Rare is the occasion when an older person is contradicted or treated with disparagement. Grandparents are deeply respected and loved, and their counsel is welcomed and valued as wisdom. Older professionals are preferred over younger ones. And there is the unwritten understanding that as parents, grandparents and even aunts and uncles grow older, the children will take care of them.

Actions that evidence this respect for age and its accompanying wisdom include day-to-day activities such as helping an older person carry things, providing assistance in crossing the street, running errands for an elderly neighbor or family member, addressing older individuals as *"usted,"* and requesting *"la bendición"* from a parent, grandparent, aunt, uncles, *padrino* or *madrina*.

DEATH AND MOURNING

Following the death of a spouse in a more traditional community, full mourning is observed for as long as several years. This includes the wearing of black clothing exclusively and a restriction on certain amusement or entertainment activities, such as dancing and movies. In other areas, mourning may extend up to two years for a spouse or a parent, and one year for a sibling. At the present time, *el luto* (mourning) is observed less intensely in many places than in the past. For example, some individuals observe *medio luto* where the observation involves only the wearing of black and white or dark colors, while others limit the time of mourning to less than a year.

However, still very common throughout the Hispanic world is *el velorio*, the custom of participating in a vigil all night by the casket of a deceased person. Although such gatherings can become quite active with food and drinks, the general tone remains one of mourning.

Practiced more in rural or lower income areas is the *velorio del angelito*, occasioned by the death of a child under the age of seven. Since the child at this age is considered innocent and thus *un angelito*, a little angel, this watch is unique in its tradition and activity. Though the parents of the *angelito* pay the expenses of the funeral proceedings, the *padrinos* (godparents) of the child generally cover the festivities of the event. This may include food, alcoholic beverages, and singers. The coffin is decorated with flowers, and a staircase is placed over it to represent the child's ascent to heaven. Some parents also place their own pictures in the coffin with the idea that their *angelito* will be paving their way to heaven.

Like *el luto*, the *velorio* has been going through some change in recent decades, especially in urban areas. Whereas formerly the event was held in the home, it has gradually moved to a local funeral home.

During the funeral in many Hispanic countries, participants maintain the tradition of walking behind the vehicle that transports the coffin. This may occur during the movement from the home to the church, from the church to the cemetery, or both. Families with greater economical resources will rent the service of a hearse, usually black or gray, while those with lesser means may use a pickup truck or other form of transportation. When the procession reaches the entrance to the cemetery, a family member, a friend, or an important civic personality often speaks about the life of the person who has died. This brief speech is known as *la despedida del duelo*.

A custom that often continues after the burial is *el novenario* or *la novena*. This nine-day period is a time for certain acts of devotion, including prayers called *rosarios* and celebrated masses.

Another typical practice following the death of a family member or friend is the custom of publicly announcing the death through the newspaper, sometimes even on the front page. These announcements include the deceased person's name along with the names of the immediate family. Since the space of the notice is a paid entry, the size tends to reflect the family's economical position. It is also very common to see notices contributed by friends, the employer, associates, or other relatives.

In the event of a death due to a murder or vehicular accident, family members of the victim sometimes erect a miniature cross at the fatal site. Most often seen by the side of the road, these crosses are constructed of wood or cement, painted white with black lettering indicating the name of the deceased person and the date of death. At some sites the crosses are sheltered by a small cement structure or are decorated with flowers, especially on the anniversary of the death.

Upon encountering a family member of someone who has recently died, a much appreciated gesture is a simple handshake followed by *"Le (te) doy mi pésame"* ("My sympathy to you"). If it is a closer friend who is grieving, though, a hug and verbal *"Le (te) doy mi más profundo pésame"* ("My deepest sympathy to you") is appropriate to show more affection and emotional involvement.

Another phrase that is often used, even after the passage of a significant length of time following a death, is *"Que en paz descanse"* ("May s/he rest in peace"). This phrase, utilized at the mention of a person who has died, conveys a respectful and appreciative tone to the conversation. If this effect is desired in writing, the initials *Q.E.P.D.* are added in parentheses immediately following the name.

2

Social Traditions

Having just arrived by plane to a Spanish-American country, I merged with the crowd of people heading toward the immigration desk. Observing the long line of people already ahead of me, I conditioned myself to expect a considerable wait. I noticed many persons in front of me involved in conversations with each other and recognized this friendly interaction as a cultural peculiarity. I silently took a place in the line behind a man, reserving a distance of a couple of feet between us.

I too was content to wait, allowing myself the opportunity to absorb the familiar sights and sounds. Significant separation from my birth culture and language had reawakened an appreciation and awareness of details that I had earlier taken for granted. I began thinking back about queues of people in other times and settings. I remembered the long lines of children I joined while waiting for lunch at school. As a young adult I often waited for business transactions at the bank and municipal offices. Then there were the lines waiting for the city buses. With so many people in towns and metropolitan areas, I reflected, waiting in line was a part of life.

At that moment my contemplation was interrupted by the motion of a well-dressed woman slipping into the polite space I had allowed between the man ahead of me and myself. Although initially surprised and piqued, I had to admit to myself that in all the remembering, I had forgotten a most significant characteristic of these queues: very close positioning.

STANDING IN LINE

Waiting in line in supermarkets, stores, banks, government offices, bus stops and at ticket windows has its own characteristics in Hispanic communities. Most noticeable is that the individuals waiting in the line stand very close together. Though it may feel too close to an outsider, any noticeable space between two persons invites occupation by someone else. Interestingly, the same situation occurs between moving vehicles in a transited area.

Another observable trait of the queue is its amiability. Though some individuals in line will be waiting silently, very often conversations are flowing easily among others. This occurs between two individuals, in clusters, and may at times even involve the entire group.

LENDING OF ITEMS

Integral to this culture is the tradition of lending and borrowing, all the way from small to very large and valuable items. A neighbor, friend, or family member may ask for a cup of sugar or for an expensive tool to fix the car. When money is lent to an acquaintance, relative, or friend, no papers are signed; only *la palabra* (a verbal promise) indicates that the money, no matter the amount, will be paid back. *La palabra* is very important and holds a lot of weight. This practice of lending and borrowing is viewed as a vote of confidence and good friendship among the parties involved.

TAKING THE *SIESTA*

As one of the oldest Hispanic customs, the tradition of taking an afternoon rest becomes a physical necessity in tropical areas where temperatures are very high during the middle of the day. In these settings, seeking refuge indoors is a must. Linguistically, since this peak also occurs around *la sexta hora,* or the sixth hour of the working day, the term has gradually evolved into *"la siesta."* In some places, businesses close for a few hours during the hottest part of the afternoon and then extend store hours into the early evening.

SPONTANEITY AND PLANNING

Spontaneity and enjoyment of the present moment are in general the characteristics of the Hispanic way of life. An impromptu visit to a friend's home or a family outing planned on the spur of the moment is preferred to detailed plans for free time.

While some societies orient themselves toward the future, this culture centers more in the present. Intrinsic is the feeling that the day which is known and experienced is worth more than the unknown future, fostering a sense of leisureliness in the rhythm of daily activities and enhancing the enjoyment of even common activities such as eating, conversing, and time with family and friends. Though influenced centuries ago by the Latin idea of *carpe diem*, "enjoy life before it is too late," the concept has affected life today for a whole society in the daily flow of activities.

VISITING FRIENDS AND FAMILY

The *visita* is a very important part of cultural life. Friends and family members freely drop in to chat for a while without previous notification. Even though visitors are welcomed at any time, the most popular time for visiting is on Saturdays, Sunday afternoons, and holidays.

The spontaneous *visitas* are very much appreciated and seen as a occasion for sharing and enjoying family, friends and acquaintances. Usually the visits are informal and the guests are served *jugo* (juice) or *café* with bread or crackers. Sometimes the visitors bring some token of appreciation such as fruits, pastries, or homemade goodies.

THE TRADITION OF THE *TERTULIA*

A *tertulia* is a very old Hispanic custom in which a group of people gather to talk about a specific topic. In practice, the same individuals generally meet every day in the same location which may be in a bar, a store, the plaza or the local pharmacy. Though the discussion can range from a friendly informal conversation to the more formal, it usually centers on literature, politics, economy, sports, culture, art, current events or things in general.

Historically the name *"tertulia"* had its beginning with Tertuliano, a Roman of the second century A.D. who was known for his eloquence. More recently, this centuries-old conversational gathering has begun to decline due to competition with the entertainment world of TVs, VCRs, video games and computers. Nevertheless, it still remains active in some large cities, and is quite prominent in small towns and rural areas.

SOCIAL NOISINESS

In public gathering places such as cafes, carnivals, game arcades, and other locales within the Hispanic world, the noise level can be quite high. In any social activity, anywhere, participants vocalize freely and loudly. Generally, this noisiness is a sign of energy, enthusiasm, or emphatic involvement in the discussion. Very often more than one person is talking at the same time and participants frequently interrupt each other, beginning to speak before another has finished. Inevitably group events become an energetic blend of sounds, gestures, and simultaneous interactions, described in some areas with the African-derived word *"la bachata."*

Without a doubt, this extroversion and verbal freedom is an integral part of the Hispanic spirit; the noisy ambiance is an accepted and even desired, side effect.

THE GUEST ROLE

When welcomed into a Hispanic home, the message to the guest, whether verbal or unspoken, is: *"Esta es su casa"* ("This is your home"). Traditional verbal greetings of welcome include *"Esta es su casa," "Están en su casa"* (literally "You are in your own home") and *"Mi casa es su casa"* ("My home is your home"). But typical hospitality goes beyond the greeting and offers a rich amount of courtesy, generosity and openness. Guests are treated as "kings and queens" and entertained with elegance within the economical resources of the host and hostess.

In response to this warm welcome a courteous guest, will upon entering the home, greet the host and hostess and shake hands with each, often presenting a small gift of appreciation, such as candies, flowers or homemade goodies. The guest will also accept any gift from the host family graciously, and if that is their desire, will open it immediately. A typical visit may extend for several hours, with each person present enjoying the richness of the moment.

As the guest is preparing to leave, the host or hostess generally opens the door. Before taking leave, the guest then expresses appreciation for the hospitality shown and shakes hands with those present. In addition, the thoughtful gesture a few days later of sending a note of thanks also reiterates the enjoyment of the time experienced together and provides another opportunity to express gratitude for the pleasurable event.

RESPONSE TO INVITATIONS

Upon receiving an invitation to go out to a restaurant, to the movies, or to a social event, it is generally understood that the one issuing the invitation intends also to pay the bill. Likewise, when friends happen to meet in a restaurant or a bar, the expression *"Yo te invito"* or *"Yo invito"* ("It's on me"; literally, "I invite you") immediately establishes who is paying the bill on that particular occasion. It is also assumed that the other person will reciprocate the next time. In the setting of a cafe or bar, common procedure is for each person to "pay a round" rather than expecting one individual to buy the beverages all the time.

With this in mind, a culturally sensitive person will not insist on paying a share of the bill when receiving an invitation to go out. Nor should the person who issues the invitation expect that the guest will even make an attempt to pay a part. This time-proven cultural custom seems to work effectively and respectfully for both the host and the guest.

UN PIROPO

An elaborate compliment or a flirtatious remark given by a male to a female who is passing by is known as *"un piropo."* Also called *"una flor"* (literally meaning, "a flower"), *el piropo* continues from a very old custom. In its truest sense, the compliment indicates an appreciation and awareness of a woman's charm and beauty. Indeed, to create a *piropo* or *"piropear"* that is appropriate to the occasion is considered an art. The woman, upon hearing the praise, is to continue on her way pretending to ignore it.

A *piropo* may be a simple *"Adiós, guapa (linda, mamacita),"* or it can be quite embellished, as illustrated by the following well-known *piropos*:

—*¡Dios mío! ¡Tantas curvas y yo sin frenos!* (My God! So many curves and I without brakes!)

—*¡Santa María! ¡Qué pinta trae la niña!* (Holy Mary! What good looks this girl brings!) In Spanish this is a play on words. The "Pinta," the "Niña" and the "Santa María" were the three ships Christopher Columbus brought to the New World.

—*Ahí va la madre de mis hijos.* (There goes the mother of my children.)

—*Si cocinas como caminas, me como hasta el pegao.* (If you cook like you walk, I would eat even the toasted rice on the bottom of the pot.)

—*San Pedro dejó las puertas del cielo abiertas y se le escapó un ángel.* (St. Peter left the gates of heaven open and an angel has escaped.)

—*Qué bombón y yo a dieta.* (What a piece of candy, and I on a diet.)

—*¡Qué ojos más lindos! Mírame, por favor!* (What beautiful eyes! Look at me please!)

—*¡Conocerte es amarte! ¡Vamos a conocernos!* (To know you is to love you! Let's get to know each other!)

—*Tiene usted más armonía que una orquesta.* (You have more harmony than an orchestra.)

—*Por usted sería capaz hasta de tener suegra.* (For you I would even be willing to have a mother-in-law.)

—*¿Qué fue su padre, hija mía? Para mí que fue escultor.* (What was your father, my dear? For me he was a sculptor.)

—*Si me dice que sí, soy capaz de encontrar trabajo.* (If you tell me "yes," I would even be willing to get a job.)

—*Que Dios te guarde y me dé a mí la llave.* (May God guard you and give me the key.) There is a play on the verb *"guardar"* in this *piropo*, meaning both "to protect" and "to store" or "to put away."

—*Cúidate de la lluvia que el azúcar se derrite con el agua.* (Protect yourself from the rain since sugar melts in water.)

Although the *piropo* has roots in a poetic and appreciated tradition, more recently the practice has degenerated in some communities, where the *piropo* used seemingly intimidates or harasses the passerby. The individual making the comment thus runs the risk of being considered crude and uneducated.

COMMENTS ON PHYSICAL TRAITS

Noticeable to a visitor to this culture is the candid manner in which the physical traits of others are observed. Characteristics upon which comments are often made include the weight of a person, eye color, skin color, hair texture, body build, physical abnormalities, and beauty or lack of it. In fact, a trait can become the base for a nickname that follows the person for life, used alone or in combination with the individual's given name: *Luis El Ciego* (Luis the Blind), *José El Feo* (José the Ugly), *El Cojo* (The Cripple), *La Sorda* (The Deaf), or *La Muda* (The Mute).

Many times these observations lead to the creation of unique comparisons that vividly illustrate the ingenuity and flavor of Hispanic humor. The following gives an illustration of a few:

—*Tiene más dientes que una peinilla.* (S/he has more teeth than a comb.)

—*Tiene más cabeza que una libra de clavos.* (S/he has more head than a pound of nails.)

—*Es más negro/a que el culo del caldero.* (S/he is darker than the bottom of the rice pot.)

—*Es más blanco/a que la leche.* (S/he is whiter than milk.)

—*Tiene más brazos que un pulpo.* (S/he has more arms than an octopus.)

—*Es más largo/a que la esperanza de un pobre.* (S/he is taller/longer than the hope of a poor person.)

3

Verbal/Nonverbal Formalities

For hours my wife and I had traveled by bus through dusty and snaking roads to visit one of the North American students participating in the Central American program we were directing. Upon arriving we found our way through the small picturesque town nestled in the mountains to the home of the host family. We were warmly welcomed with the traditional greeting of a handshake, an embrace and *"Entren, ésta es su casa."* Soon we were sitting around the supper table, our plates filled with delicious food typical of the area. Conversation flowed as *don Manuel* and *doña Josefina* shared news of their small town, spoke of their projects and employment, talked about their grown children and growing grandchildren, and remarked how well Mary—*"María,"* they called her—was adjusting. We were finishing up with the *cafecito* when Mary, while shifting her sitting position, accidentally kicked *don Manuel* in his leg. I could see that she was mentally searching for the correct vocabulary to excuse herself. Her subsequent choice of *"Con permiso, Papá"* brought a slight flicker of confusion to *don Manuel's* face though a few seconds later he graciously responded, *"No hay problema."*

Later when we were alone with Mary, I referred to the incident at the table, aware that it was a teachable moment. Together we explored the different uses of *"con permiso"* and *"perdón,"* and laughed as she realized that a choice of *"Perdón, Papá"* would have been more appropriate.

GREETINGS

A noticeable characteristic of the Hispanic social setting is the warm, friendly, and affectionate interaction, especially evidenced in the way in which people greet each other. Indeed, the degree of respect and warmth shown as a person meets and greets another is very important in this culture. And since the greeting is valued so highly, it tends to be more elaborated, prolongated, and ritualistic.

The handshake is very basic to the process of greeting. Friends and acquaintances, from adolescence up, shake hands upon meeting and again when leaving. And even though the handshake is done with the right hand, the left hand can send an extra message of warmth and affection when placed over the other's hand and giving a gentle squeeze. This is known as *un apretón*.

Besides the handshake there are additional nonverbal ways to communicate warmth in a greeting. Male friends often follow a handshake with one or two pats on the back, while very good friends give one another *un abrazo* (embrace or hug) followed by several slaps on the back. Women generally embrace and exchange *besos* by touching cheeks and kissing the air. A man and woman may embrace and kiss on the cheek, but only if they are relatives or close friends. When a man and a woman shake hands, the man will bow his head or his upper body slightly—a gesture of politeness originating in the old custom of bowing to kiss a lady's hand—and direct eye contact is made.

When greeting people, expressions denote different degrees of formality or informality. Phrases of greeting used informally with friends and peers include:

—*¿Qué tal?* (How's it going?)
—*¡Hola!* (Hello!)
—*¿Cómo te va?* (How is it going with you?)
—*¿Cómo estás?* (How are you?)
—*¿Qué hay de nuevo?* (What's new?)
—*¿Qué pasa?* (What's happening?)
—*¿Qué me cuentas?* (What's new to tell?)

Meanwhile *"¿Cómo está(n) usted(es)?"* ("How are you?") is more formal and is used with acquaintances, older people or superiors. Some typical responses to these greetings, in order of formality, are *"Bien, ¿ y Ud./tú?"* ("Good, and you?"), *"Regular," "Así así"* ("So-so"), *"Más o menos"* ("More or less"), *and "Pues ahí"* ("Alright").

When two friends pass on the street, they may stop, shake hands, and then talk for a while. If they do not intend to stop and talk, their greetings may be a simple *"¡Hola!"* ("Hello") or *"¡Adiós!"* ("Goodbye") accompanied by a friendly raising of the hand, which indicates a respectful acknowledgment of the other's presence. A verbal greeting is culturally expected. In fact, to fail to do so may be taken as an offense, and the person not extending the greeting considered arrogant.

Addressing People

In addressing another person in formal settings, titles such as *licenciado, señora,* or *señor* are regularly used rather than the first name. It is also quite common for the marital status of *señor, señora,* or *señorita* and a professional title to be combined when addressing an individual: *Sr. abogado (lawyer), Srta. profesora, Sra. doctora, Sr. ingeniero,* or *Sra. maestra.* In addition, a university professor who holds a doctoral degree may be appropriately addressed as either *doctor(a)* or *profesor(a)*, though the latter is used more frequently.

Introductions

In introducing one person to another or to a group, the introductory phrases used are the informal *"Te presento a . . ."* and the formal *"Quisiera presentarle(s) a . . ."* Following this verbal presentation, the individuals involved always shake hands and give their names followed by expressions like *"Mucho gusto," "Mucho gusto en conocerlo/a," "Encantado," "Encantado de conocerlo/a," "A las órdenes," "Tanto gusto," "Un servidor," "Para servirle," "Es un placer,"* or *"Es un placer conocerlo/la."* All of these expressions give the idea of "It is nice to meet you."

As in the greeting, the physical action of shaking hands is essential to communicate warmth, sincerity, and the pleasure of meeting. A mere nod of the head, wave of the hand, or a quick "Nice to meet you" does not carry this message adequately.

Icebreakers

For persons who are not very well acquainted, the type of courteous questions used to start conversation flowing after the introduction is generally of a less personal nature. Preferred as icebreakers are topics such as community events and activities; the person's occupation; the size of one's family and the whereabouts of family members; sports, music, art, and literature interests. Questions about family affairs or a spouse's occupation are considered too personal for this level of acquaintance. Though the topic of politics is an appropriate entrance into conversation as well, caution should be taken to avoid expression of one's personal views or comparison of the country's political practice with one's own.

FAREWELLS

Despedidas or farewells do not have as many variations as greetings. Often people will shake hands and use the expression *"Hasta luego"* ("See you later") to which is given the response *"Si Dios quiere"* ("God willing"). Other common farewell phrases include:

—*Hasta lueguito.* (See you soon.)
—*Hasta la vista.* (So long.)
—*Que Dios te bendiga.* (God bless you.)
—*Chao.* (Good-bye.)
—*Adiós.* (Good-bye.)
—*Hasta pronto.* (See you soon.)
—*Nos vemos.* (We'll see you.)
—*Cúidate.* (Take care.)
—*Que Dios te acompañe.* (God be with you.)

COURTEOUS EXPRESSIONS

Of important value in the Hispanic culture is the ability to express oneself in a polite manner when dealing with others. Practicing courtesy and respect, even when inconvenienced, touches the essence of this culture. Polite expressions go beyond words or phrases, since underlying the spoken is an acknowledgment that the personal space of another has been approached, and so respect and appreciation are merited.

Some common expressions of courtesy used frequently include:

—*Lo siento (mucho).* (I am [very] sorry.)
—*Gracias.* (Thank you.)
—*Muchas gracias./Un millón de gracias./Mil gracias.* (Thanks a lot.)
—*De nada./Con mucho gusto./A la orden./A las órdenes.* (You are welcome.)
—*Por favor.* (Please.)
—*Mucho gusto.* (I am please to meet you.)

—*Bienvenido.* (Welcome.)
—*Felicitaciones./Felicidades./Enhorabuena.* (Congratulations.)

There are several expressions in Spanish that are used to say "Excuse me": *"Con permiso," "Perdón,"* and *"Por favor."* The phrases are not interchangeable since each one carries its own connotations. They are discussed in more detail below since English speakers may have some difficulty with their usage.

"Con permiso" is the expression used when passing in front of two people conversing, when leaving a group, when turning one's back on someone, or when eating in front of a person who is not eating. Literally it asks another's permission to proceed with an action or to interrupt. The response to this request is *"Concedido"* ("Granted").

"Perdón" or *"Perdone,"* meanwhile, is another way of saying "Excuse me" in the event of an accidental action that affects another person, such as bumping into someone or stepping on a person's foot. Here one is making an apology or asking for pardon. The appropriate response in this case is *"No hay problema"* or *"No hay de que"* ("No problem").

"Por favor," which also means "Please," is also used to say "Excuse me." This expression is utilized to get another's attention or to politely initiate a request for assistance or information: *"Por favor, ¿podría Ud. decirme dónde queda la farmacia?"* ("Excuse me, could you tell me where the drugstore is?").

Compliments

In a conversation when a compliment is given, a sensitive response will convey the idea that the giver of the compliment was very kind and that the receiver is happy for the enjoyment experienced. Some frequently used responses to compliments include *"Me agrada que le guste"* ("I am glad that you like it"), *"Es muy amable de su parte decirme eso"* ("It is very kind of you to tell me that"), *"Verdaderamente aprecio sus comentarios"* ("I truly appreciate your comments"). Responding with a simple *"¡Gracias!"* or *"¡Muchas gracias!"* in response to a compliment is not as suitable, since it communicates in this culture that the receiver of the compliment thinks the praise was deserved.

On the other hand, compliments should be given simply. Excessive admiration or repetitive praise of an object owned by another may lead the owner to respond, *"Tome. Es suyo."* ("Have it. It's yours."). In the event that a gift results from a compliment, a gracious response is to accept the gift as a valued possession and to show appreciation.

Asking Favors

In asking a favor, the simplest way is to use the imperative or command form in conjunction with the phrase *"por favor"* ("please"). This is placed either at the beginning or end of the sentence in order to soften the effect.

—*Deme eso, por favor.* (Give me that, please.)
—*Levante la mano, por favor.* (Raise your hand, please.)
—*Por favor, envíe la carta.* (Please send the letter.)

However, since the command form in some situations may sound too brusque, another technique is to use the present tense, the conditional tense, or the verb *"hacer"* followed by *"el favor"* in the format of interrogative sentences.

—¿*Me presta su revista?* (Would you lend me your magazine?) [present tense]
—¿*Puede Ud. darme el libro?* (Can you give me the book?) [present tense]
—¿*Podría firmarme el documento?* (Could you sign the document for me?) [conditional tense]
—¿*Tendría inconveniente en manejar más despacio?* (Would you mind driving slower?) [conditional tense]
—¿*Me hace el favor de no comer en el salón de clase?* (Would you do me the favor of not eating in the classroom?) [*hacer* + *el favor*]

Though these examples use the formal *usted* form, the informal *tú* could be also utilized to create a more friendly mood. In addition, the purpose of the conditional tense *podría* and *tendría* in the third and fourth examples is to provide a degree of politeness or formality to a situation where the granting of the request is not automatically assumed.

However, in those events where an affirmative answer is almost certain, a commonly used phrase or word is often inserted at the end of the request.

—*Compra el pan, ¿está bien?* (Buy the bread, all right?)
—*Ve a la famacia, ¿quieres?* (Go to the pharmacy, would you?)
—*No grites tanto, ¿de acuerdo?* (Don't scream so much, would you?)
—*Vende el bate, ¿sí?* (Sell the bat, OK?)

Expressions of Gratitude

Agradecimiento or gratefulness is expressed in a variety of forms. If the action is simple such as having the door opened or lending a pen, gratitude is merely expressed with a *"¡Gracias!," "¡Muchas gracias!,"* or *"¡Muchísimas gracias!,"* or if more affect is desired, *"¡Mil gracias!"* (literally "A thousand thanks!")

At another level, if *el favor* (the favor) is much greater, such as lending a car or piece of equipment to one in a difficult situation, the response is frequently *"¡Que Dios te lo pague!"* ("May God pay you back!") or *"¡Que Dios te bendiga!"* ("May God bless you!"). Likewise, gratitude is often expressed through a gift such as a dish of *arroz con dulce* or a crocheted *tapete* (doily). *"Tú me haces un favor a mí y yo te hago uno a ti"* ("I do you a favor; you return me a favor") is such an integral part of the cultural expectation that favors are rarely, if ever, repaid with money.

4

Nonverbal Communication

The student knocked at the door, and upon my invitation entered my office. He said he wanted to talk with me about a report he was writing for the literature course I was teaching.

"I think I have a book that will help you in this," I told him after hearing his specific request. "It is over there."

The student looked at me first, and then with a slightly confused expression on his face, his eyes darted around the room. Since I had told him the book was "over there" I was a bit puzzled at his response. So again I proceeded to indicate the location of the book on my office shelves.

As I saw his surprised eyes focused on my mouth, I suddenly realized that while I was trying to express an idea in a nonverbal way understood by my culture, the message was not communicated when crossing cultural lines. Through my ancestral connections, I had learned that even though lips are mainly for talking, eating, kissing, and such purposes, when pursed in a directional manner with an accompanying lift of the head, lips could also communicate location. For my student in this setting, I was rapidly learning, I would need to define "over there" differently.

GESTURES

Gestures are integral in the Hispanic culture where hand and body movement and facial expression hold an essential role in communication. Gestures are not only used to accompany words, but also to replace them, sometimes telling more than the verbal.

Some gestures are used universally for communication, while others vary from culture to culture. In fact, sometimes an acceptable gesture used in one society or setting may be offensive in another. One illustration of this in the United States is the light pat to the buttocks by teammates when a baseball player has made a good play. In other settings, and especially within the Hispanic culture, this would not be acceptable. Another acceptable gesture in the United States culture is the "OK" sign, where the thumb and index finger form a circle while the other fingers face outward. This symbol of communication is obscene in the Hispanic world. For this reason, it is wise to be informed about appropriate gestures for a given occasion or culture.

Some gestures that are well known to the Hispanic world in general follow:

1. **To describe a skinny person:** Make a fist and raise the little finger.
2. **To indicate that there are a lot of people:** Hold hand with palm up. Close hand until the fingers touch each other.
3. **To describe a person who is stingy:** Bend forearm upward, not far from the body. With cupped palm of the other hand, softly tap the bent elbow.
4. **To show that one must be careful and alert:** Place the tip of the index finger under the eye and pull slightly downward.
5. **To indicate that someone is very angry:** Bend the elbows, putting both hands up, shoulder height, then curve the fingers in a claw shape facing outward.
6. **To describe "excellence":** Put the tips of the five fingers of a hand together. Kiss them, and while moving the hand away, spread the fingers.
7. **To communicate "just a moment" or "just a little bit":** Hold the hand in front, palm down. Bend the last three fingers toward the palm while extending the index finger and thumb parallel to each other, with about an inch of space between the index finger and thumb. Or, hold the hand in front with the palm facing sideways. Bend the last three fingers toward the palm while extending the index finger. Place the tip of the thumb about one inch down below the tip of the index.
8. **To show that two people are very good friends:** Extend the right and left index fingers parallel to and touching each other while bending the other fingers.
9. **To describe the act of eating:** With palm of hand up, bend fingers toward the thumb. Holding this position, move the hand back and forth toward the mouth. The mouth can be either open or closed.

10. **To portray money:** Place palm facing up with the index and middle fingers together. Then rub the thumb of the same hand over the tips of these two fingers.

11. **To emphatically affirm or swear:** Place the index finger behind the thumb with the last three fingers slightly raised and away from the index-thumb combination. Kiss the thumb. Often the phrases *"¡Por la madre de Dios, te (se) lo juro!"* or *"¡Por mi madre, te (se) lo juro!"* accompany this action. These phrases are equivalent to the English "I swear before God" or "I swear on my mother's grave."

12. **To warn someone not to release information:** Place the tip of the tongue between the teeth, usually to the side. Touch the tongue with the index finger.

13. **To express a "so-so" situation:** Place hand with palm facing down, fingers spread, and elbow close to the body. Shrug the shoulders, lean the head toward the hand making the gesture, and tip the hand from side to side.

14. **To communicate "No!":** Face palm of hand upward and out. With thumb and middle finger touching, index extended and remaining fingers bent, move hand from side to side at the wrist.

15. **To indicate that two people are at odds with each other:** Touch the tips of the right and left index fingers, forming a horizontal line.

16. **To express the act of consuming alcoholic beverages:** Close the hand with extended thumb toward the mouth. Move the hand in this position and the forearm toward and away from the mouth.

17. **To describe that someone is "crazy":** Tap the side of the head several times with an extended index finger.

18. **To instruct someone to "come here":** Hold the forearm up with the palm outward and somewhat inclined. Move the fingers up and down repeatedly.

19. **To show the height of a person:** Place palm of hand facing down, bending it slightly down at the wrist. Lift arm to the desired height.

20. **To show the height of an animal or object:** Place palm facing down. Stretch out the arm and raise it to the desired height.

21. **To show the length of an object the size of a machete or knife:** Extend the left arm and place the tips of the right-hand fingers on the inside of the left-arm elbow area. For an object much longer, the right-hand fingers are placed on the left arm/shoulder area. Usually accompanying this gesture of measurement is the expression *"Era así de largo"* ("It was this long").

BODY LANGUAGE

Body language is very important in cross-cultural communications, and like other cultures, the Hispanic society holds certain expectations and practices of nonverbal communication. The classroom as a fairly formal setting is a good illustration of several cultural expectations and interpretations of body language.

In the classroom it is expected that a student's feet remain on the floor, not resting upon adjacent tables or chairs. Except in very informal situations, tables, desk tops, floors, and counter tops are not used for sitting either. These actions along with refraining from slouching or scooting low into the chair during class time all give a positive nonverbal message of involvement with the course material and respect for the teacher and the ambiance of the classroom. The message of mutual respect is also shown when small items such as papers, pens or books are individually handed to peers, the teacher, or a student rather than informally tossing it to the person. In fact, in the Spanish-speaking world, the act of tossing things in a social setting is considered very rude.

Eye Contact

To communicate interest and sincerity during conversation, direct eye contact must occur. Similarly, in conversations within a very small group, a speaker will attempt to make eye contact with each participant. Repeatedly overlooking a group participant potentially conveys an intent to ignore.

On the other hand, there are times when eyes should be lowered. When a child or adolescent faces someone in authority, such as a parent or teacher, or is being disciplined, a lowering of the eyes indicates respect. It is helpful to be aware of this in a cross-cultural setting, since in other cultures lowered eyes can be mistaken for showing guilt or not paying attention.

Staring

When discovering something or someone new, it is acceptable within the Hispanic culture for the observer to display interest and curiosity by staring. This may involve a slightly prolonged glance or a study *"de pies a cabeza,"* from "head to toe." To an outsider who may be the object of scrutiny, this produces a certain degree of discomfort or annoyance. Understanding that this action is merely a cultural peculiarity with no specific reason or alternative intention removes the temptation to take it as a personal offense.

Turning One's Back

Though the act of turning one's back on someone, or *"dar la espalda,"* may be done unwittingly, the individual in the Hispanic culture is very intentional about correcting such a situation. During a group conversation when a speaker suddenly realizes that someone is standing behind, s/he will immediately turn around, address that individual with *"Perdón,"* and then continue speaking with obvious inclusion.

Sneezing

When a sneeze is heard, the person who has just sneezed says *"¡Perdón!" "¡Salud!"* ("Health!") comes the response from those nearby.

There are of course variations to this cultural routine. *"¡Jesús!"* is the expression of blessing sometimes bestowed upon the individual who has sneezed. A regional variation often heard in Puerto Rico is *"¡Dios lo (te) bendiga!"* ("God bless you!"). And a fun response to those who sneeze several times in a row is: *"¡Salud!"* ("Health!") after the first sneeze, *"¡Dinero!"* ("Money!") after the second, *"¡Amor!"* ("Love!") after the third, with *"¡Y tiempo para gastarlos!"* ("And time to spend them!") as a conclusive note.

Yawning

To *bostezar* or yawn is a part of being human, especially when one is tired, bored, sleepy, or under extreme stress. Openly yawning is not considered culturally appropriate, however, so in the process of a yawn, the mouth is covered as discreetly as possible, and at times an apology such as *"¡Perdón!"* ("Pardon!") or *"¡Disculpe(n)!"* ("Excuse me") is also given.

5

Ways to Address People

On the day my parents carried me to the baptismal font, I became *Angel Rafael Falcón Meléndez Vázquez Rosario*, a seemingly huge name for a very little boy. My parents had decided upon the middle name in honor of my uncle, *Rafael*, who had raised my father after the death of their mother.

During my childhood this name was shortened to *"Rafo."* In fact most people in my Latin American hometown knew me as such, many of them unaware that my name was really *Angel Rafael*.

It was years later that my christened name suffered a most significant blow when I enrolled in a North American university for graduate studies. Accustomed to signing my name as *Angel Rafael Falcón Meléndez*, I decided to drop the *Meléndez* since university personnel was assuming it to be my official last name. Shortly after, I also eliminated the *Angel*. While considered to be a very common male name in my birth culture, it was a woman's name in this new place of residence. Telemarketing employees would rapidly discover that the "Angel" in our house was, in fact, me.

My name acquired new status, however, during a year of residence in Costa Rica. In that time I was addressed as *"don Rafael,"* a title of respect. Although I was still young, the title was given to me because of the administrative position in which I was employed.

FIRST NAMES

In this culture children are usually given more than one *nombre de pila* (baptismal name; literally, baptismal font name): Alfredo Miguel or Carmen Ana, for example. Sometimes a name is given based upon the saint's day on which the child is born, but more often children are named to honor another member of the family, a good family friend like a *padrino* (godfather) or *madrina* (godmother), or simply because a name sounds appealing. More recently, many families are moving away from the traditional names of Pedro, Pablo, María, or Teresa, to names with a English flavor or background like Walter, Nelson, Janine, and Betty.

Some names in this culture are borrowed or adapted from religious tradition. Use of the name *Jesús* is not uncommon for men, and at times *Juan de Dios* (John of God) is used for a male child. Similarly, some female names are short forms of titles given to the Virgin Mary: Concepción, Carmen, Pilar, Consuelo, Rocío, Guadalupe, Virgen, Providencia, Amparo, Pura, Santa, Piedad. This, in reality, parallels the practice in other cultures of using names such as Hope, Faith, Charity, Chastity, Grace, and Prudence.

A few male names are actually masculinized forms of names generally used for females: Carmelo from Carmen, Mario from María. At times, too, female names such as Dolores, Guadalupe, and María are given to men, though María, when used for a male, is usually in the format of a middle name: José María or Jesús María, for example. In turn, some names for women are forms of names more often used for males: Jesusa from Jesús, Josefa from José. Male names are also occasionally used for women as a middle name: María José.

Some names seem to be favorites, commonly used and appearing through the generations. Pedro, Juan, or Antonio for men and Ana, Carmen, or María for women are examples. If two individuals have the same first name, each may refer to the other as his/her *"tocayo(a)."* It is a relationship based purely on the name, and is expressed as *"Somos tocayos(as)"* ("We are *tocayos[as]"*) or *"El/Ella es mi tocayo(a)"* ("S/he is my *tocayo[a]"*).

Several other customs related to this topic are distinct for this culture. Rarely are persons called by their first two initials; no one would be called T.R. Meléndez, for example. In addition, to differentiate between a father and a son who have the same first name, the word *padre* or *hijo* (father or son) is inserted after the first name, as in *"Rafael, padre"* or *"Rafael, hijo."* Also, a descriptive phrase utilizing a parent or relative's name is sometimes inserted after a first name in order to provide helpful identification: *"Rafín el de tío Monche," "Carmen la de doña Ana."* And finally, in some Hispanic regions when the article *"la"* is utilized with a female first name, it is done intentionally to show strong dislike of the person or to emphasize socially unacceptable behaviors: *"La Juana," "La Petra."*

LAST NAMES

Two *apellidos* (last names) are used in this culture: The first last name comes from the father's surname, *apellido paterno*, and the second from the mother's last name, *apellido materno*. To illustrate this, the son of Ramón Miguel *Sáez* López and Providencia Rosa *Falcón* Vázquez has as his name Héctor Manuel *Sáez Falcón*. Sometimes only the first last name (the father's) is used with the second one abbreviated: Héctor Manuel Sáez F. However, both surnames are required for legal purposes. In fact, in some instances, such as birth registrations, all four last names are used in an alternate manner: Héctor Manuel Sáez Falcón López Vázquez.

In Spanish there are many *apellidos* ending in "ez." Historically, the ending showed that an individual was a descendent of the person to whose name the suffix was attached. Thus, a man named *González* was the son of *Gonzalo*, or one named *Rodríguez* was the son of *Rodrigo*, very similar to the English names ending in "son": Peterson, Emerson, Christianson, Ericson, Johnson. Some of the many Spanish last names ending in "ez" include Alvarez, Benítez, Domínguez, González, López, Martínez, Meléndez, Núñez, Pérez, Rodríguez, Vázquez, Velázquez.

The names or descriptions of animals, vegetation and flora, religion, geometry, and the human body have also provided the foundation for last names. This is illustrated in the following:

Origin	Last Name	Translation
Animal		
	Becerra	Calf
	Cerda	Female pig
	Toro	Bull
	Vaca	Cow
	Cordero	Lamb
	León	Lion
Vegetation/Flora		
	Flores	Flowers
	Naranja	Orange

	Robles	Oaks
	Limón	Lemon
	Rosas	Roses
	Melón	Melon

Description of the Human Body

	Delgado	Skinny
	Barriga	Stomach
	Prieto	Black
	Gordo	Fat
	Moreno	Black/brown
	Rubio	Blonde
	Cabezas	Heads

Religion

	Iglesias	Churches
	Rosario	Rosary
	Santa	Saint

Geometric Shapes

	Redondo	Round
	Cuadrado	Squared
	Agudo	Sharp

In addition, many last names are created by using the preposition *"de"* ("of "): *de Jesús, de León*. Or the *"de"* is combined with another preposition *"la"* ("the"): *de la Torre, de la Garza, de la Madrid, de la Hoz*.

Some *apellidos* can also be used as first names. Examples are Domingo, Santiago, Juan, Guadalupe, Santa, Cruz, García, David, resulting in an occasional individual having the same first and last name: Santiago Santiago. Most of these interchangeable names can be traced to religious origins.

When a woman marries, she usually keeps both of her last names and adds her husband's first surname. Thus, if Providencia Rosa *Falcón Vázquez* marries Ramón Miguel *Sáez* López her name becomes Providencia Rosa *Falcón Vázquez* de *Sáez*. She could then be addressed as *la señora de Sáez* or simply *la señora Sáez*. The couple and their children would be known as *los Sáez*.

A widow who wishes to use her late husband's surname may use *Vda. de,* coming from *viuda de* (widow of), after her last name: Petronila Rosario Vda. de Meléndez. A woman never uses her husband's first name as part of her name. This means that a Hispanic woman would not be addressed as *la Sra. Manuel Alvarado* (Mrs. Manuel Alvarado).

The system of two last names creates a problem for Hispanics living in the United States since the maternal last name shown as the second surname is mistakenly thought to be the main one, whereas the paternal, the first surname, is assumed to be a middle name. Persons caught in this situation sometimes opt for solutions such as hyphenating the last names, *Sáez-Falcón*, or dropping the maternal last name, *Héctor Manuel Sáez*.

NICKNAMES

Nicknames known as *sobrenombres* or *apodos* are often used in place of first names. Thus, *Rafael* becomes *Rafo, Rafa, Rafín* or *Rafín* and *Cristina* is known as *Tina*. Some common nicknames for a person's given name include:

For males:
- Francisco - Paco
- Guillermo - Guillo
- Enrique - Quique
- Ramón - Monche
- José - Pepe
- Ignacio - Nacho
- Eduardo - Lalo
- Antonio - Toño
- Manuel - Manolo

For females:
- Guadalupe - Lupe
- María Luisa - Marilú
- Dolores - Lola
- María - Mari
- Graciela - Chela
- Mercedes - Meche
- Teresa - Tere
- Concepción - Concha

Sometimes a nickname is based upon a characteristic trait of an individual. As examples, *el Cojo* may be used to refer to a person who limps, *el Ciego* to an individual who has sight problems, or *el Chato* to one with a flat nose.

On the other hand, *apodos* are sometimes used for purely affectionate reasons. Common examples include calling a sibling or good friend a *"gordito(a)"* or *"flaquito(a)"* when in reality that person is not "chubby" or "skinny," or calling one's spouse *"negrito(a)"* for reasons not related to skin color. Another common nickname showing affection for one's father is *"mi viejo,"* literally "my old man."

At other times, nicknames are based upon the trade of a person: *Pedro "El Zapatero"* for a man who is a shoemaker or *Pablo "El Carnicero"* for a butcher named Pablo. In fact, some of the nicknames become so related with the person that the real name may be forgotten.

The most common nicknames end in "ito" for boys and "ita" for girls. Alfredo, Marcos, and Camilo become Alfredito, Marquitos and Camilito; while Ana, Juana, and Teresa become Anita, Juanita, and Teresita, respectively. If it is desired to use the whole name plus the nickname, the *apodo* can be incorporated into the name: *Francisco "Paco" Martínez* or *Pedro "El flaco" Rodríguez*. Another way to involve the nickname with the given name is to use the term "alias," as for example, *Pedro Rodríguez, alias "El flaco."*

A word of caution for newcomers to the culture: Observe the practice of others. Even before substituting a commonly used nickname for a name, be perceptive. An example is *"Toño,"* which though often utilized for *"Antonio,"* is not used for all males with that name. Likewise, the informality of generic nicknames such as *"pana," "viejo,"* or *"compadre"* (equating "buddy" or "pal") may offend someone if used inappropriately.

"John Doe"

When it becomes necessary to refer to a person whose name is either unknown or forgotten, names such as *Fulano, Mengano, Perengano* or *Zutano* are used. Occasionally these "John Does" are referred to in a longer form: *Fulano de Tal, Mengano de Tal.*

SEÑOR, SEÑORA, SEÑORITA

The Spanish equivalent of Mr., Mrs., and Miss are *Sr. (señor), Sra. (señora),* and *Srta. (señorita).* And even though the title *"Señor"* traditionally refers to the "man of the house," its use in the plural as *señores* can allude to several men, to the equivalent of "sirs," to a collective group of women and men, or to a married couple such as *los señores Meléndez.* The term *"Señora,"* meanwhile, may address a married woman of any age, any woman of middle age or older whose marital status is unknown, or "the woman of the house." *"Señorita"* refers to any young woman who is single or whose marital status is unknown, and even though the English title of address "Ms." has no direct equivalent, either *"Señorita"* or *"Señora"* parallels its use, depending upon the general age of the woman addressed. Meanwhile the title of *"Señorito,"* though used in past centuries for the unmarried male, is rarely used today. In a situation where the name of an individual is unknown and yet one needs to call the attention of another, the title of *"Señor,"* *"Señora,"* or *"Señorita"* is used alone.

DON AND *DOÑA*

Don is a term of respect used for addressing a man; *doña* for a woman. Each precedes the first name of an individual: *don Pedro* or *doña Ana*. *Don* originates from the Latin masculine noun *dominos* meaning "lord," "master," "head of a household," and *doña* is derived from the feminine noun *domina* signifying "lady," "lady of the house."

Originally titles of nobility, these terms now show respect to someone of higher social or professional position or to an older person. *Don* and *doña* signify a relationship closer than a *señor* or *señora* level, but yet not intimate enough for a first-name basis. While *don* can be used to address or refer to any man, single or married, the use of *doña* is limited to married or widowed women. A single woman, regardless of her age, is shown respect through the title *"señorita."*

Appropriate to this culture is the practice of combining at times the terms *don* and *doña* with first and last names including occasionally the titles of *"señor"* or *"señora."* Examples include *"don Pedro,"* *"don Pedro Rodríguez,"* *"Sr. Dn. Pedro Rodríguez,"* *"doña Ana,"* *"doña Ana Valdés,"* and *"Sra. Dña. Ana Valdés."* *Don* and *doña* can be combined with *señor* or *señora* when addressing a letter, invitation, or document, to show closeness to the person addressed with appropriate appreciation and respect. Neither *don* nor *doña*, however, is used in combination with a professional title.

TÚ, USTED, AND *USTEDES*

When we address someone, well known or otherwise, in English, we use only one pronoun "you." Spanish speakers, meanwhile, need to choose between addressing a person informally with the pronoun *"tú"* or formally with *"usted."* And since the use of these two terms has complex sociolinguistic implications that are difficult to reduce to a set of specific rules, the following guidelines may assist understanding:

—The Use of Tú: The informal pronoun *"tú"* is used to address peers, children, friends, a person of the same social position, close acquaintances, or pets. It is also utilized with God to help create an atmosphere of closeness between God and the person praying. The use of *"tú"* is called *tuteo;* to use it with somebody is to *tutear.*

—The Use of Usted: The formal pronoun of direct address is *usted*, which is abbreviated *Ud.* or *Vd.* This is reserved for people whom one does not know as well, who are older, or who are in a formal occupational position such as a boss, doctor, lawyer, professor, or police officer. Customs sometimes vary in some countries in the use of this formal pronoun. The word *usted* comes from the old Spanish term *"vusted,"* which in turn developed from *"vuestra merced"* ("your grace"; literally, "your mercy").

Most Spanish speakers do not distinguish between informal (familiar) and formal (polite) addresses in the plural. Thus *ustedes*, which is abbreviated *Uds.* or *Vds.*, is used with everyone.

Misuse of either the formal or informal "you" can create an uncomfortable situation. To address someone as *"tú"* when *"usted"* should be used may imply less respect. On the other hand, to address an individual as *"usted"* when *"tú"* would be more appropriate, creates an element of separation. In a setting where one is uncertain which "you" should be used, it is best to go with *"usted."* If the addressed person prefers the *tuteo* relationship, s/he will likely inform the speaker, thus eliminating any misinterpretations.

VOS

In Argentina, Paraguay, and Uruguay; in parts of Colombia, Chile, and Ecuador; and in most of Central America, Spanish speakers use *"vos"* instead of *"tú,"* though use of *"tú"* is perfectly understood. *"Vos"* is a form of respect that was widely spoken in the past. The use of *"vos"* is called *"voseo,"* and the action of addressing someone with *"vos"* is to *"vosear."*

Except for a few verb forms, such as the present tense indicative and subjunctive, for example, the *"vos"* verb forms are almost identical to those conjugated with *"tú."* As an illustration, verb conjugations with *"vos"* in the present tense take this format: *hablás, querés, escribís.*

VOSOTROS

"Vosotros" and *"vosotras"* are the grammatical plurals of *"tú,"* used only in the northern and central areas of Spain to address two or

more people with whom one has a friendly relationship. The terms originate from *vos* (you) and *otros* (others).

As mentioned earlier, in Spanish America the plural of *tú* is *ustedes*, whether the context is formal or informal (familiar). So any distinction between formal and informal in this part of the Hispanic world is made only in the singular with *tú* or *usted*. Spain differs by using the formal and informal in both the singular and the plural: the singular *usted* and *tú* and the plural *ustedes* and *vosotros(as)*.

DEFINING *"AMIGO"*

The concept of *amigo* in Hispanic countries has a slightly different connotation than the English word "friend." *Amigo* signifies an intimate, trusting, deeper relationship that lasts a lifetime and could better be translated as "close friend." Out of a group of *amigos* there are probably one or two who are even closer. These are considered to be *amigos íntimos* (intimate friends).

An individual with whom one associates on a more casual yet regular basis is considered one's *conocido(a)* (acquaintance), *socio(a)* (associate), or *compañero(a)* (companion). The latter term is used more in contexts such as *compañero(a) de clase* (classmate), *compañero(a) de cuarto* (roommate), and *compañero(a) de trabajo* (co-worker).

DEFINING *"HISPANO"* OR *"LATINO"*

Hispano or *Latino* are terms used to refer to the people and cultures of Spanish-speaking countries. The term *hispano* is more specific for the Spanish heritage, since it refers only to the people who speak Spanish and who come from the historical Spanish background. *Latino*, on the other hand, is linguistically broader, including all people from a Latin American background whether they speak Spanish, French, Portuguese, German, English, or indigenous dialects. Both terms, however, indicate the cultural background of an individual, not necessarily the place of birth. Hispanics born within the United States illustrate this cultural connection: Puerto Rican Americans, Mexican Americans and Cuban Americans are considered *hispano* and *latino* despite their birth in the United States.

DEFINING RESIDENTS OF THE UNITED STATES

The term used to designate residents of the United States varies from country to country in the Spanish-speaking world. *"Americano(a),"* *"gringo(a),"* *"norteamericano(a),"* and *"estadounidense"* are all terms used to describe this group of people. Some regions use one more than another, yet as is detailed in further discussion, each term proves somewhat inadequate as a describer.

The term *"americano"* is an illustration of this problem. Heard frequently to define this group of people, the term is in fact a misnomer since all people from the Americas are "Americans."

As an alternative, the term *"gringo(a)"* is used in some places such as Puerto Rico, Venezuela, Colombia, Perú, Costa Rica and Dominican Republic. While the terminology is useful in these countries, it becomes problematic in other countries, such as Mexico, where *"gringo(a)"* has derogatory connotations.

In other Spanish-speaking countries such as Argentina and Spain, people from the United States are called *norteamericanos*. However, this term also applies to individuals from Canada or Mexico who are sharing the North American continent.

Yet another descriptor is *estadounidense*, a word based on the phrase *estados unidos* (united states). Though this phrase is somewhat confusing because of its use in the names of several other countries in the Americas such as Mexico and Brazil, it is still used to refer specifically to the United States of America. *"Estadounidense"* is most frequently used in formal language settings: in books, classrooms, lectures, written formats, and newscasts.

All of these terms are viable descriptors of residents of the United States. Of these *"norteamericano(a)"* and *"estadounidense"* tend to be less problematic, presumptuous, and more specific.

6

Family and Household Relationships

"Bendición," I called out from my bed after the lights went out in the house.

"Dios te bendiga," answered the comforting voices of my parents from their bedroom.

"¿Me cuidas?" I continued.

"¡Claro, hijo!" was the reassuring response.

So went the nightly ritual for me as a boy growing up on a Caribbean island. But the tradition of *"bendición"* followed by *"Dios te bendiga"* also enriched our daily relationships as we left and returned from our typical activities: a day at school, a trip, even beginning and ending a telephone conversation with a parent, grandparent, aunt or uncle.

At times the benefit of the tradition transcended the emotional and spiritual. There was the day downtown when my father introduced me to my *padrino*, a good friend of his whom he called his *compadre*. Coached by my father, I extended my hand to shake that of my *padrino*, while verbally requesting from him the respected *"bendición."* To my delight, as I heard the familiar *"Dios te bendiga,"* I also felt the cool hardness of a coin tucked into my palm. Later requests for the *"bendición"* proved my padrino to be creative; sometimes I received a coin, or a piece of candy, or even a dollar bill.

THE BLESSING

Originating in traditional Spanish culture, *la bendición* (the blessing) is still practiced in some Hispanic countries as an integral part of greetings and farewells among family members. Upon entering and leaving a home, for example, younger members request *la bendición* from their parents, grandparents, uncles and aunts, and godparents by saying, *"La bendición, papi (abuela, tío)."* The older person will then reply, addressing the individual, *"Que Dios te bendiga, José"* ("God bless you, José"). Sometimes money or candy accompany the blessing for the younger child. In those countries where this is still practiced, the older members of the family expect that the younger generation initiate the ritual, whether on the street or in the home.

THE FAMILY UNIT

In much of the Hispanic world, the basic family unit extends beyond the nuclear grouping of father, mother and children to include grandparents, uncles, aunts, cousins, godparents, and even *compadres*. Here it is common for extended family members, known as *los parientes* or *los familiares* (relatives), to live in the same household as the nuclear family. And within this culture, the most important social unit to which a person belongs is *la familia*, the extended family.

As the family unit matures, parents generally expect their single, adult children to live with them while they attend college, until they get married, or until they find a job away from home. Although in the larger cities customs are slowly changing, adolescents and young adults do not usually leave the parental home to live by themselves.

The family is also the refuge for the older members, and it is not uncommon to have two or more generations living together under the same roof because of cultural, practical, and economical realities. Grandparents prefer to live with their children rather than in a retirement or nursing home. And since they often take care of the younger children while parents are at work, there is a reduced need for *niñeras* (baby sitters). *Los abuelos* (grandparents) enrich the family unit by passing onto the children and grandchildren the traditions taught to them by their parents. At the same time, this contact with the older generations helps the younger members to absorb helpful attitudes, manners, language, duties, and other essentials of a culture. Without a doubt, grandparents play a very important role in the Hispanic family system.

Family ties traditionally remain strong even after children leave home. Since a particular bond to each other and a strong sense of loyalty to the family has been established, when family members travel, they are expected to stay with relatives rather than in hotels. And just as family members are welcomed into the homes of their extended family, so are their friends. Maintaining strong connections is extremely important: Family is a source of emotional and material support when needed.

For the children who marry, this extended-family culture has even provided vocabulary to describe the relationship between the two sets of parents of the married couple and between the two sets of siblings of the spouses. The relationship between the parents of the husband and those of the wife is known as *consuegros* (*con* = with; *suegros* = joint in-laws). And with a marriage, the brothers and sisters of the husband have a new relationship with the siblings of the wife; they are now *concuñados*, joint brothers/sisters-in-law.

Since tradition is strong in the majority of Hispanic families, the husband is generally considered the head of the family, while the role of the wife is to keep the house in order, to care for the children, and to manage the kitchen duties. In some places, especially in the larger urban areas, these roles have been changing as women pursue careers or work in a wide variety of jobs outside the home.

Due principally to industrialization of the economy, the family is now undergoing some change. As young people from small villages and rural areas move to cities in search of better paying jobs, the nuclear family becomes more prevalent. In some situations both the husband and wife hold jobs. These fast-paced changes have been producing alterations in a culture where traditionally the male has held the main role as economic provider and where family members have benefited from the support of the extended family system.

THE ROLE OF CHILDREN

Children in the this culture grow up surrounded by a large circle of family members. Grandparents and unmarried adult relatives frequently live in the home, while uncles, aunts, and cousins often live nearby. The need to employ outside childcare is uncommon since extended family members (or servants for the wealthier families) are available.

It is common to observe children, even infants and toddlers, participating with family members in restaurants, religious services, and movie theaters. Adults are usually very tolerant of the occasional disruption and noise generated by children.

In speaking with each other, parents and children generally use *tú*, the informal form of "you." In some rural areas and in some countries such as Colombia and Guatemala, though, children address their elders as *usted*. In general, in speaking with their children parents usually reserve the *usted* form for those situations in which they wish to make greater emphasis in a statement.

FAMILY GATHERINGS

Throughout history, family gatherings have played an important role in the social life of the Hispanic culture. Mealtimes provide a chance for family members to assemble at least once a day and to share the events of their separate lives. On Sunday, married children regularly take their spouses and children to visit their parents and to eat together. On occasions such as weddings, baptisms, Christmas, Easter, *quinceañeros* (a young woman's fifteenth birthday celebration), and religious or national holidays, relatives get together for family reunions and parties. These family gatherings provide valuable opportunities to make connections and renew ties.

Traditionally, there is an unwritten understanding that adult children will attempt to visit their parents several times a week. If this is not possible because of distance or for business reasons, at least a phone call is expected.

COMPADRAZGO

Derived from the influence of the Catholic religion, one of the oldest and most important customs in the Hispanic culture is *el compadrazgo*, the relationship between parents and godparents. The liaison begins at the time of baptism when the child receives spiritual parents, known as *padrinos* or godparents. Usually, the godparents are members of the child's family such as an uncle or aunt, though sometimes they can be close friends of the family. They do not need to be married to each other. These two people, *la madrina* (godmother) and *el padrino* (godfather), provide security for their *ahijado(a)* or godchild, assuming the spiritual and economical responsibility of the biological parents in the event of crisis or tragedy within the family.

Children may have different *padrinos* for other sacraments, such as the first communion, confirmation, marriage, or ordination to the priesthood. However, the most important set of *padrinos* are those who are chosen to take responsibility for a child and who share in the baptismal event.

Emerging out of the terminology of this important custom, and yet completely apart from it, is the current usage of the terms *compadre* and *comadre*. Literally meaning co-father and co-mother, *compadre* and *comadre* are used in the context of "good friend," "associate," or "companion."

THE MAID

It is common for families in many Hispanic countries to employ a maid. This employee sometimes lives with the family and helps the woman of the house with the household chores: grocery shopping, answering the phone, meal preparation and serving, child care, laundry, and more. If a maid has been with the family for many years she may be considered part of the family. Some of the more prosperous Hispanic countries have recently faced challenges finding this type of household help. As a result many of the middle- and upper-class families are meeting their needs through the employment of a person for only several hours per week.

If a maid is in the home, guests are expected to treat her and the other household help with considerable reserve. For example, the maid is not to be requested directly to do things for them, unless they have first asked the *señora* of the house. Especially in the area of kitchen work, guests are not expected to clear the table, take plates to the kitchen, and so on. This is considered the domain of the maid and the *señora de la casa* and should be done only after discussing this with the hostess, in deference to the established roles of the household.

The terminology used for the word "maid" varies from country to country. While *"criada," "sirvienta," "muchacha de servicio,"* and *"empleada doméstica"* are understood throughout the Hispanic world, there are areas where *"criada"* and *"sirvienta"* may have derogatory connotations. Other names for "the maid" are more regional: *"mucama,"* used in Uruguay, Chile, Peru, and Argentina, or *"empleada"* in Costa Rica.

7

Gender Issues and Relationships

I heard it from my friend that Carmen Ana, an attractive seventeen-year-old classmate of mine, had told him that she liked me. I liked her too. So after some time of friendship and conversation, we decided we wanted to be *novios*. Since I was the male it was up to me to initiate that status, so I asked her, *"¿Quieres ser mi novia?"* Although both of us knew each was interested in the other and Carmen Ana wanted to be my *novia*, she also knew how to "play the game" and took her time in answering me. Of course, a reasonable period of time is expected for responses to such questions, and she eventually accepted.

Now we were ready to set the perimeters for our relationship. It was mutually understood that neither of us would date anyone else. I also had some specific expectations for her: I did not want her to wear tight slacks, shorts, or lipstick. She agreed to honor my preferences.

Among our peers we were recognized as *novios*, and we both enjoyed this special relationship at school and away from home. But Carmen Ana wanted our relationship to be known and accepted by her parents so that I could visit her in her home. In other words, she wanted me to *"pedir la entrada a la casa."* To make this happen I would need to be introduced to her parents and would need to ask them if I could visit her in her home; they would then determine the times I could visit.

At that point, this seemed too great of a commitment for me, so I made the tough decision to break off our relationship.

Although this was my choice, many of my friends did *"pedir la entrada a la casa"* of their female friends. As long as those relationships lasted, I knew I could not be with them on weekend evenings from 7–10; those were the traditional visiting hours in the homes.

DATING

Dating in the Hispanic society is initially group oriented. Beginning around the ages of fourteen or fifteen, teenagers go out in groups with their friends, acquaintances and classmates. Separation of the group into couples usually happens near the end of the high school years.

Courtship

Once the young couple has made a more serious emotional commitment to each other, the term *novio(a)* is used. This term implies a deeper and more serious relationship than "boyfriend" or "girlfriend," and holds very clearly defined expectations for the young man and woman. Known as *el noviazgo*, the time of courtship begins with a declaration of love. After hearing her friend formally *declararse*, the woman is given time to accept his request; the couple will then date only each other. If the young man wants to visit his *novia* (girlfriend) in her home, he is expected to speak with her parents to ask for visitation hours.

In some places a *chaperón*, who is often a friend of the family or a relative, is expected to accompany the couple. If they plan to be alone in the home of one or the other to watch a movie, to eat or have a drink, or to study together, other persons are to be present with them. For either one of them to give or accept an invitation to be together without others around gives the message of a desire for sexual intimacy.

When the young woman is escorted to the entrance of her home after a date, it is seen as preferable in most Hispanic countries that she invite her *novio* into the house rather than to have a long good-bye at the front door. This eliminates the need for the neighbors to have any reason to comment and saves the family embarrassment.

The general norms of courtship behavior have eased a bit more recently, yet a decision to enter *el noviazgo,* while involving both, still affects the young woman more. The expectation for her to consult with *su novio* on most aspects of her life can alter considerably her former independence. In some situations the freedom to talk with other males may even be limited, unless she and her *novio* are together. Depending upon the couple's personality, even minor aspects of her life such as wardrobe, makeup, or manner of speaking, as well as more consequential choices like study abroad or a job change, can be influenced by the male. Believing that this behavior shows that he cares, the young woman often accepts and conforms to this involvement in her life.

Expectations and changes for the young man are less restrictive. If his *novia* is more assertive, he may also lose some liberties such as going out with his friends or participating in certain activities. However, this is not as common in this culture, since men traditionally have more freedom than women.

It is customary for the man to ask the young woman's father for her hand in marriage. Family usually plays an important part in the choice of marriage partners, since the new member will be an integral part of the whole family unit. *Un compromiso* or engagement period of several years' duration is common.

THE MARRIAGE EVENT

In some Hispanic countries marriage requires both a civil and a religious ceremony. The civil ceremony is a relatively brief event held at the courthouse, usually preceding the religious celebration. The religious ceremony is generally held at a church and is attended by family and friends.

With a more formal religious ceremony, a bridal party is often part of the marriage celebration. Accompanying the couple as members of the bridal party are a *padrino, madrina, caballeros,* and *damas.* The *padrino* is either the father of the bride, a male friend of the family or a relative, while the *madrina* is the mother of the bride, a female friend of the family or a relative. The *caballeros* and *damas* are usually friends of the couple. If the wedding includes a traditional Catholic mass, there will also likely be a *padrino* and *madrina de velaciones*, whose role is to place a veil and a string over the couple, symbolically uniting them.

Another unique element in some wedding proceedings is the tradition of *las arras*, which are thirteen gold coins. As part of the ceremony, the groom gives these coins to the bride. Of Germanic origin, the word *"arras"* signifies a guarantee of responsibility in a contract or transaction. In this context, then, the coins represent commitment to the marriage. Even though this custom is not practiced in all Hispanic countries, it is still an important part of the formal marriage ceremony in Mexico and Spain.

After the wedding ceremony newlyweds often live with the parents or in-laws until they are able to afford their own apartment or house.

Divorce in some parts of the Hispanic world has increasingly become a more accessible option. But even though it is possible in these countries, a divorce is as yet not easy to obtain, and often carries negative social sentiments, especially in areas where the influence of the Catholic church is very strong.

MALE GENDER ROLES

Even though traditional male and female role expectations are slowly changing in the Hispanic world, certain responsibilities and activities are still considered more appropriate for one gender or the other. Mechanic-type work, for example, is more "suitable" for a man; conversely, household chores such as cooking, cleaning, and washing dishes are considered more appropriate for a woman.

Men are raised with the idea that they are to provide food and shelter and protect the women in their lives, be they sweethearts, sisters, mothers, daughters, or spouses. Their world is away from home: work, sports, social gatherings. Men are also allowed certain social freedoms that are not culturally accepted for women, for example, going out to a bar at a very late hour.

Machismo

It is difficult to examine the roles of men and women in the Hispanic society without mentioning the impact of machismo. Throughout history, as young boys in this culture grow to adulthood, they experience the myth that the true mark of masculinity is to demonstrate courage, virility, and male domination. This erroneous and exaggerated understanding of maleness, commonly known as *machismo*, conceptually stems from the Middle Ages. The term itself is a derivative of the Spanish word *macho*, meaning male.

Machismo manifests itself in a variety of ways. Examples include reducing women to a passive and submissive status; attempting to convince others of one's bravery through the use of defiant gestures and words; stoically enduring injury or illness while refusing medical attention; having repeated sexual conquests; fathering many children, often with different mothers; needing to excel in physical activities, especially fighting; and obsessively praising one's own masculinity.

Obviously, being a *macho* carries strong sexual overtone. A man who is *macho* in the most radical sense of the word shows society his "masculinity" by having sexual encounters, even going as far as fathering a child just to leave a "trophy" of his conquest.

Without a doubt, *el machismo* puts unnecessary cultural pressure on young boys to conform as they are developing their attitudes and actions towards other males and towards females.

Alcohol and Maleness

To measure up to the traditional *macho* ideal, one must drink. Accordingly, excessive drinking permeates the Hispanic male culture. Alcoholic beverages are consumed at weddings, parties, baptisms, and funerals; often any occasion will suffice. Sometimes a *fiesta* is improvised to create an occasion to drink, or a work project invented more for the alcohol than to accomplish the task. Though consumption happens any day, the favorite celebration time with male friends is Friday after work, known as *viernes social.*

For the maturing young man the pressure to drink is very strong, and there is little support for those who choose to violate this cultural norm. Thus, the male who does not drink fears being viewed by his peers as physically ill, a coward or a religious freak. The *real* man, it is erroneously believed, is the one who can consume the hardest liquor in the greatest quantities without being affected by it. And a favorite activity among some groups of men is a race to empty the most cans of beer or bottles of wine.

"Don Juan"

As mentioned previously, *el machismo* manifests itself in a variety of ways. One of these is the characteristic known as *"un tenorio,"* or "Don Juan" to English speakers, a term that describes a seducer of women. The name is derived from the hero of the seventeenth century play entitled *"El burlador de Sevilla"* ("The Seducer of Seville") by Tirso de Molina, a work that has served as the basis for later writings by several well-known authors including Zorrilla (Spain), Molière (France) and Lord Byron (England). While the infamous hero's complete name is Don Juan Tenorio, only his last name is utilized as a synonym in Spanish for such a type of man.

FEMALE GENDER ROLES

The traditional role expectation for the married woman, meanwhile, is to be devoted to her home and the care of her children, faithful to her spouse, and religious. If the father is absent from the home, the mother becomes the center and base for the ongoing activities of the household. As women are entering the working world outside of the home, the traditional roles and expectations of both men and women are changing. This is especially true as women are entering professional and managerial positions.

Marianismo

Derived from the biblical *María* (the Virgin Mary), *marianismo* describes an attitude of extreme self-sacrifice and humility displayed by many women, especially those of middle age and older. In essence, *marianismo* is an attempt of these women to rationalize their resignation to the reality of male dominance and female submission in their personal lives. The suffering endured for the sake of children and husband is the "cross" they carry, albeit with bitter pride, providing self-worth in the eyes of God, the family, and the community. To be known as *sacrificada* (self-sacrificing) is a compliment, giving meaning to a response of understanding and patience, for example, when a husband is unfaithful or a child has problems with the law. By such a wife and mother, the stories detailing this reality are told repeatedly to any interested listener. Tied into this mindset is the cultural view of a maternal image as a saint, extremely patient and sacrificial, and ultimately venerated by the entire family.

Understandably in a society where *machismo* and *marianismo* are realities, the marriage in which the wife appears to be the dominant figure is criticized and ridiculed by both sexes. Proverbial sayings provide tongue-in-cheek illustrations of the tension between those roles fixed by cultural expectations. Supporting the status quo mentality is the saying *"El gallo canta; la gallina solamente cacarea"* ("The rooster sings; the hen only cackles"), while the following sayings humorously describe relationships where the wife seems to be more dominant:

—*Lo tienen sentado en el baúl.* (They have him sitting in the trunk.)
—*El hombre dice la última palabra: "Sí, nena, lo que tú digas."* (The man has the last word: "Yes, dear, whatever you say.")

—*El hombre es la cabeza del hogar, pero la mujer es el cuello que mueve la cabeza.* (The man is the head of the home, but the wife is the neck that moves the head.)

8

Religious Issues

In the 1950s my father was a neighborhood leader in the Catholic church for our *barrio, El Roble*. As part of his responsibilities he was in charge of organizing the church activities during special occasions, such as *Semana Santa* among others. He would always say he was Catholic, but in reality I had never seen my father attend church on a regular basis.

Around that time, a Protestant group from the United States came to the island and established several churches, a couple of schools, and a hospital. As part of that presence, my family was invited by some neighbors to attend the new church in our area.

I can still remember that first Sunday when my father, mother, sister, brother and I dressed in our good clothes and drove in our car to the small simply designed concrete church with two palms in front. It was a day of contrasts for me since I was old enough to remember the few times our family had together attended the ornately constructed Catholic church located on the edge of our town's plaza. The participatory nature of the worship of that tiny congregation was attractive to our family, everyone sang together, there were classes for us children, and the sermon was in our own language. We had been accustomed to the mass spoken in Latin, which we could not understand.

After that first visit, my family gradually became more and more involved with the congregation. My siblings and I were enrolled in the school organized by their denomination. Soon my parents found themselves at a crossroads of decision-making: to identify with the Protestant church would put them at odds with the faith of their cultural roots, as well as set them apart religiously from their family connections.

RELIGIOUS DIVERSITY

When speaking of religion, the Hispanic world is almost always considered Catholic. It is true that a great majority of the population, perhaps over 95%, are baptized into the Catholic faith in these countries. Yet there is also religious diversity present. Even within the Hispanic Catholicism there is evidence of non-Catholic religious influences both in the hierarchy and at the popular level. Illustrative of this conglomeration of diverse religious beliefs are those areas of greater Indian populations, such as in Mexico, Central America and the Andean region. Here religious practice combines attributes of the Catholic saints with characteristic of the gods evolving from ancient Indian religions. Similarly, in the Caribbean countries, some African practices and beliefs have mixed with traditional Catholic observances.

In recent years there has been an increasing growth in religious groups outside the Catholic church. Those with the greatest success are usually the evangelical Christian denominations having connections with the United States. Specifically, the Pentecostal and modern charismatic movements have made great strides. Characterized by spontaneity and emotionality in the singing and preaching, the worship of these congregations appeals to and meshes well with the natural emotional nature of this culture. In addition, healing services, exorcisms, and being "slain in the Spirit" contribute toward meeting the spiritual and emotional needs of the participants. Even though these denominations and congregations are still a small minority, they are growing rapidly and do represent a dimension of the religious diversity within the Hispanic world.

THE ROLE OF WOMEN IN RELIGIOUS PRACTICE

In practice, the religious life of the Hispanic culture is dominated by women. Though the hierarchy of the church is male, women carry out the everyday instruction and inspiration. Society does not expect the father in the home to be highly religious, so an appearance in the local congregation at Easter, Christmas or on a special occasion is considered normal. On the other hand, the mother or wife is the religious statement of the family; it is her role to instill faith in her children and take them to church. Thus traditionally in this culture, it is the woman who creates the credibility, respect and veneration for the religious life of the society.

VISIBLE RELIGIOUS EXPRESSIONS

Intertwined into the daily rituals of many individuals is the visible expression of religious preference, faith, and emotions through the use of signs and symbols. An athlete, for example, will unabashedly *persignarse* or make the sign of the cross before taking on a challenge, whether stepping into the batter's box, entering the boxing ring, or getting into position in a marathon. But even outside the athletic arena, the *señal de la cruz* is a ritual performed by anyone during typical events, before leaving for a trip, or when observing a potentially tragic or unfortunate event.

Another visible expression of religiosity is the use of medallions or chains that contain a religious image, or the wearing of a rosary. Religious images are also displayed in cars, buses, and taxis. While some home owners place a statue of a saint in front of the house or on the porch, others hang a large picture of Jesus or the Virgin Mary in the living room, dining room or bedroom.

RELIGIOUS PROMISES

Closely connected to the way many people practice their religion is the making of *promesas* (promises) in a bargain with God for a desired outcome. Often these promises are visible and intended to cause inconvenience for the promise maker. For example, the wearing of *un hábito* (a certain habit) for a year may be the promise made in hopes that a spouse be healed from a terminal disease, although the material is heavy and thick and the climate may be tropical. Another example is a mother in distress over the status of a child injured in an accident who creates the *promesa* to walk on her knees for miles to a specified church. A very common action is the decision to refrain from cutting one's hair or beard for a designated period of time.

The execution of these promises is more common in some countries than in others. Yet they remain a real and vivid part of the Hispanic way of practicing religion.

RELIGION-BASED EXPRESSIONS AND SAYINGS

Routinely in this society, many expressions of excitement, volatility, surprise, emotion, and volition use words evolving from the Christian tradition. *"Dios," "María," "Jesús,"* and the names of saints are often used. In fact, some of the most frequently spoken exclamations, liberally translated, include

—*¡Dios mío!* (My gosh!)
—*¡Ave María Purísima!* (Holy Mary!)
—*¡Por Dios!* (For Pete's sake! / Holy Cow!)
—*¡Válgame Dios!* (God help me!)
—*Con la ayuda de Dios.* (With the help of God.)
—*¡Sabe Dios!* (Only God knows!)
—*Dios mediante.* (God willing.)
—*Si Dios quiere.* (God willing.)
—*Que Dios te acompañe.* (God be with you.)
—*¡Ay, Bendito!* (My goodness!)
—*¡Jesús!* (Wow! / My goodness!)

Used within the Spanish language setting, these interjections are not considered offensive or blasphemous. In most cases the terms are now devoid of any true religious meaning, serving instead as a vehicle to communicate certain emotions. In fact, many persons using these expressions are devout churchgoers.

Apparent also are the many common sayings that show a clear influence of the Roman Catholic Church. If someone is not liked very well, an appropriate saying is *"No es santo de mi devoción"* ("He is not saint to whom I pray"). If someone has become distracted and forgotten something: *"Se me fue el santo al cielo"* ("The saint left me and went to heaven"). Of somebody who "robs Peter to pay Paul," the phrase *"Desnuda a un santo para vestir a otro"* ("Undress one saint to robe another") refers to the special garments commonly used to clothe the images of the saints. In some communities, if there is a robbery and everything is stolen, the saying used is *"Se fue con el santo y la limosna"* ("S/he took off with the saint's image and the offering for the poor").

SANTERÍA

Common in several Caribbean countries is *la santería,* a religious practice where gods of African origin exist side by side with the Christian saints. The term *santería* comes from *"santo,"* which means "saint." Practitioners are called *santeros* in general, while the female practitioner is known as a *santera.*

Historically, when the Spaniards brought African slaves to America the newcomers were forced to adopt the Christian religion. The slaves, however, continued with aspects of their own religious beliefs, thus ultimately creating a fusion of religions. Illustrating this syncretism is the honored *Babalú* who corresponds to the Catholic saint Lazarus, the protector of people who are ill, or *Changó* who equates St. Barbara, the patron saint of firefighters and the protector from lightning, as well as many other gods.

Although there are special symbols and rituals associated with each god, practices vary from one country to another. One example of a spiritual ritual practiced in some countries is that of sacrificing chickens, goats, or doves to a particular god, especially as a treatment for depression and other emotional illness.

9

Supernatural and Superstitious Beliefs

My energetic eighty-eight-year-old maternal grandmother had as usual walked several miles from her house to visit our family. For me, *Abuela's* visits were always awaited with great anticipation. Besides being dependably there for me with support and caring wisdom, she would also usually bring items for my instant gratification: favorite candies such as *dulce de coco, mampostiales, ajonjolí*, or appreciated fruits in season like *pumagasas* or *guayabas*. This ritual, of course, served only to endear her even more to me.

This time, though, *Abuela's* visit was especially significant for me. I was now twenty-six years old, married, and eager to introduce my recently born first son to this very important woman in my life. *Abuela* arrived; the *"bendición"* was requested and the *"Dios te bendiga"* received. The goodies were distributed to my younger siblings, and then *Abuela* picked up and cradled my small son in her arms.

Time ceased as I observed those wrinkled hands caress the tiny soft hands of my son. She commented on his big blue eyes; she said he was a very beautiful child. Then she pulled from the wisdom of her age: "Purchase," she instructed me, *"'una manita de azabache'* to pin onto his tiny shirt. A great-grandson of mine so attractive needs protection from *'mal de ojo'.*"

My grandmother's life had been filled with the hard work of raising nine children in a small home without modern conveniences. She had never had the opportunity to learn to read and write. Experience and tradition were her education, which had apparently served her well. It was from this background that she was now instructing me to buy a small amulet, carved from lignite into the shape of a closed hand, which she believed would protect my son from the effects of an "evil eye."

SUPERNATURAL BELIEFS

In most of the Hispanic countries, belief in the supernatural exists in a very real way. Malicious spirits, goblins, demons, witches and appearances of the Virgin Mary characterize a world that co-exists with the natural. Supernatural powers may be invoked when a drought threatens the crops or an epidemic kills the cattle. Especially in rural areas, healers known as *curanderos(as)* sell amulets for good luck, prescribe magic potions for any occasion, forecast the future, and offer advice on strategies for acquiring a husband with good potential or a wife with a promising inheritance. The power of *mal de ojo* (evil eye) or the action to *echar un fufú* (cast a spell) are important to this belief system.

One very common belief is that the souls that have not been able to enter paradise are condemned to wander on earth at night. So if a person is killed instantaneously and unable to receive the last rites, his/her soul returns to earth to avenge the murder. These souls in agony are the source of many stories and legends that are used to discourage undesirable behavior in children.

Physical healing also occurs through believed supernatural events. In some communities a specific site is converted into a sanctuary where it is said the Virgin Mary has appeared. As people travel to these areas, stories are told of miracles. Fatal diseases are cured, sight is restored, and individuals can again walk. Crutches and other paraphernalia are left behind, symbolic of restored health.

These supernatural experiences continue. Periodically the media will report another out-of-the-ordinary event: a wooden statue of Jesus with tears emanating from one of his eyes, the image of the Virgin suddenly present in the bell tower of a church, or the outline of the Virgin temporarily visible on a wall.

This play between the natural and the supernatural has been captured and creatively developed through the imaginations of several famous Latin American writers like Gabriel García Márquez in *One Hun-*

dred Years of Solitude and Isabel Allende in *The House of the Spirits*. Known as "magical realism," it has reached other media through films such as "Like Water for Chocolate" *("Como agua para chocolate").*

SUPERSTITIONS

Many superstitions in this culture are integrated so subtly into the daily life experience that they become part of the wealth passed on from one generation to the next. The following gives a sampling of the variety:

1. Placing one's purse on the floor will cause one's money to go fast.
2. Because bad spirits hover close to the ground, it is better to sleep in a higher bed.
3. A black butterfly flying around a house or a person signifies that there will be a death in the family.
4. Sweeping another's feet will keep the individual from being married. This should be avoided, therefore.
5. Breaking a mirror implicates seven years of bad luck. To reverse this curse, one must get rid of the mirror immediately, or better yet, dig a hole in the ground and bury it.
6. Seven years of suffering come to the person who kills a black cat.
7. Walking under a ladder brings bad luck. This can be remedied by crossing one's index finger over the middle finger.
8. Itching hands are a sign that money will be forthcoming.
9. A breech presentation at birth signifies a prosperous life for the baby.
10. A ringing in the left ear indicates that someone is talking badly about oneself; the comments are good if the ringing is in the right ear.

Other actions that are believed to produce bad luck include:

1. To see several nuns together on the same sidewalk where one is walking.
2. To open an umbrella inside the house.
3. To spill salt on the table or drop a piece of bread on the floor.
4. To get out of bed with the left foot first.
5. To encounter a black garbanzo bean in a bowl of stew.

Some events are believed to create good luck:

1. To attach a horseshoe to the door of one's residence.
2. To find a clover with four leaves.
3. To knock on wood three times when mentioning a wish.

Left-Handedness

Centuries of folklore and superstition have also contributed the idea that the dominant use of the left hand implies a proclivity to bad luck or a tendency to exhibit a mischievous spirit. Understandably, in some communities even today *los izquierdos* or *los zurdos* (left-handed persons) are forced to use the right hand.

Equally alive today are some idiomatic expressions or sayings that carry these superstitious messages: *"Los zurdos no van al cielo"* ("Lefties do not go to Heaven") or *"Con un zurdo/a no me caso yo"* ("With a lefty I will not marry").

"Tuesday the 13th"

Similar to the superstitious "Friday the 13th," "Tuesday the 13th" is considered to be the day of bad luck in Spanish-speaking countries. For this reason, the English-language horror movie "Friday the 13th," when translated into Spanish, was renamed *"Martes 13."* The rationale for *martes,* or Tuesday, as an unlucky day in all probability stems from the fact that the name *"martes"* is derived from Mars, the Roman god of war. And war, accordingly, signifies death.

The belief in Tuesday the 13th as an unlucky day has created folk sayings and advice. Clearly illustrating this is the well-known saying *"Martes, ni te cases, ni te embarques, ni de tu casa te apartes,"* which counsels "On Tuesday, don't get married, don't go on a trip, and don't leave your house." Additional advice for this day is to refrain from certain activities such as moving, or cutting one's hair or fingernails. Indeed, the folkloric importance of this day appears during some New Year's Eve forecasts, when the announcer mentions the months of the new year containing a Tuesday the 13th.

The connection of the number thirteen to unlucky events has both religious and historical roots. One religious version relates that there were thirteen individuals with Jesus the night of the Last Supper, and that the thirteenth person was the one who later betrayed him. Another suggests there were thirteen individuals, including Jesus, together the night before his betrayal.

Meanwhile the historical basis for Tuesday as an unlucky day rests on the fact that on Tuesday the 13th in 1453 the Byzantine Empire surrendered to the Muslims. Since this event opened a new period of Muslim power and political leadership in Europe, it was understandably considered unlucky by the Spaniards of the time.

10

Religious Holidays and Activities

The morning before the long-anticipated Three Kings' Day dawned cloudy and rainy. How, I wondered dismally, was I to gather the grass for the Three Kings' camels if it was going to rain all day? Impatiently I waited long hours of seemingly incessant showers.

Finally by mid-afternoon the rain ceased and the tropical sun shone down on a refreshed earth. With vivid pictures in my mind of the important visitors coming with their hungry and thirsty camels that night, I hurried toward a neighboring vacant lot where I jerked out a handful of grass. Then it was back to my house to place the grass, still damp from the rain, into a shoe box I had hidden away for this purpose. And my mother's storage cabinet had just the right-sized container for a bit of water for thirsty camels.

It seemed like a very long time until bedtime. But just before I jumped into my bed that night, I carefully placed the shoe box with grass and the container of water under the bed. While I was sleeping the Three Kings could come; their camels could eat and drink; and they could then continue on their very long journey. Of course, the Three Kings would be grateful for the manner in which I had cared for their camels, so they would leave a small gift to thank me.

Early the next morning I awoke, and while rubbing the sleep from my eyes, I suddenly remembered: Today was January 6, the long-awaited Three Kings' Day. I jumped from my bed

and reached under for the water container. It was empty.
With mounting excitement I pulled out the shoe box. Gone
was the grass and in its place was a shiny toy car! How did the
Three Kings know that was just what I wanted!

MAIN RELIGIOUS HOLIDAYS

Most holidays in the Hispanic world either originate in or are centered
around a religious event. Some of these are celebrated regionally while
others are enjoyed nationally or by the entire Hispanic community.
Because distinct forms of religiosity are so much a part of the culture,
the celebration of these religious holidays is integral to the society.

The main religious holidays celebrated by the Hispanic community
include:

Día de los Reyes Mago/Epifanía (Day of the Magi/Epiphany, on January 6)
Miécoles de Ceniza (Ash Wednesday)
Semana Santa (Holy Week)
Domingo de Ramos (Palm Sunday)
Jueves Santo (Holy Thursday)
Viernes Santo (Good Friday)
Día de Pascua (Easter)
Día de Todos los Santos (All Saints' Day on November 1)
Día de los Muertos/Día de los Difuntos (All Souls' Day on November 2)
Nochebuena (Christmas Eve)
Navidad (Christmas)

Día de los Reyes

In the tradition of most Hispanic countries, *los Reyes Magos* (The
Three Kings/Magi/Wise Men) pass through neighborhoods on the sixth
of January, *Día de los Reyes*, on their way to visit Baby Jesus. According to the legend, the visitors Gaspar, Melchor and Baltasar arrive at
night by camel and leave gifts for the children on porches, in windows,
or under beds. Children prepare for the event by filling a shoe box with
grass and a container with water for the camels, and the next morning
discover presents beside the emptied containers.

Another tradition of this day in some countries involves baking a
cake in the shape of a circle, known as *rosca de Reyes*. Hidden within
the cake is a small figurine, and the person discovering it while eating is
expected to host a party for his/her friends some days later.

Miércoles de Ceniza

The main event on *Miércoles de Ceniza* (Ash Wednesday) for members of the Roman Catholic Church is a mass culminating in a ritual in which the priest with his finger dipped in ash draws the sign of the cross on participants' foreheads. This symbolic tradition initiates the period of Lent, which continues for forty days and is a time for many Hispanic Christians to observe a period of prayer, penance and abstinence. Done in commemoration of Jesus' forty-day fast in the wilderness, participants of *Cuaresma* (Lent) refrain from eating red meat in their daily diet, replacing it with fish cooked in a variety of ways. A favorite dish served during this time in some places is *gazpacho,* which uses dried codfish and is prepared with onions, olives, laurel leaves, and other spices. Although the practice of refraining from certain activities during the period of *Cuaresma* has declined somewhat in the last several decades, it continues to be observed quite faithfully in some communities.

Semana Santa

One of the most important and impressive religious holidays is *la Semana Santa* (Holy Week), celebrated the week before Easter Sunday. Cities and towns are transformed during this time and many people decorate the interior of their homes with crucifixes, flowers, statues of their patron saint, and violet-colored cloths that symbolize the mourning of the crucifixion of Jesus.

On *Viernes Santo* (Good Friday) often a slow and silent religious procession winds through the streets of the town. Men wearing violet-colored penitential clothing carry heavy platforms decorated with statues of Jesus Christ, the Virgin Mary, and biblical scenes. In addition, on Good Friday some communities hold a re-enactment of Jesus' last days. During these activities there is a tone of sadness and solemnity.

On the Saturday prior to Easter Sunday, some Hispanic communities burn dolls depicting demons or representing Judas, the apostle who betrayed Jesus. In other communities a doll symbolizing Judas is paraded around town on a horse, providing opportunity for people to hit it with a stick.

Semana Santa is celebrated with such intensity that normal activities are kept to a minimum. Regular routines of going to work, shopping, making transactions in the bank, and receiving mail either slow down or come to a halt as shops, businesses, banks, and the post office close or have limited hours.

El Día de los Muertos

Important to this culture is also *El Día de los Muertos* or *El Día de los Difuntos* (All Souls' Day) on the second of November, a day for specifically remembering people who have died, and a special time to reflect that life is a movement toward death. Death is viewed as a stage in the cycle of life which need not be feared, and also an inescapable event at which one can laugh. It is a day set apart to show respect for loved ones who have died and is an occasion for festivity instead of sadness.

Of all the *Día de los Muertos* events celebrated throughout the Hispanic world, the most well-known is held in Mexico. In this country the celebration usually begins with a special mass attended by family members, who then go to the cemetery. Here they clean and decorate the graves, eat a meal together, and remember the good times they have enjoyed with those who are no longer living. Meanwhile in the homes, altars are created and decorated with gifts and a candle representing each deceased family member. Incense, food, drink, candles, or flowers are prepared as offerings. One of the special foods enjoyed during this occasion is *pan de muerto*, a sweet bread made in the form of skulls, bones, or skeletons.

Also on this day children receive "toys" made of paper or sugar that have been shaped into skeletons, skulls, and miniature coffins. Some children dress as *muertos* (skeletons or ghouls) and carry bowls to collect candies. Older ones climb into fake coffins and are carted around town. People throw the "corpse" money, candy, and marigolds, the flower of the dead.

Other traditions have evolved for this designated day, peculiar to a specific area. In Spain, for example, in addition to visiting the cemetery, participants attend the play *"Don Juan Tenorio"* at night because of its plot, which includes scenes of life beyond the grave. More recently the play has been incorporated into television programming specifically for this day.

In the Hispanic culture, children are actively included in the activities of *El Día de los Muertos*. They also attend the *velorios* and burials of family members and friends of the family, learning that death is a natural stage of life.

Navidad

La Navidad, Las Navidades or *Las Pascuas* (Christmas) is celebrated with vigor, intensity, and color throughout the Hispanic countries. During this season, which is enjoyed from early December to January 9, traditional carols called *villancicos* are sung. Tasty dishes typical of a given area are prepared: *tamales* in Central America and Mexico; *pasteles, lechón asado* and *arroz con dulce* in Puerto Rico. And alcoholic beverages such as *rompope* are mixed and served. Groups go from house to house providing *una parranda* for friends, complete with music, dance and food. Displays of *nacimientos* (nativity scenes) and *pesebres* (manger scenes) appear inside homes, in residential patios and in business areas. And families in Mexico re-enact the search of Mary and Joseph to find lodging through *"posadas."*

Nacimientos. During this season many families set up *un nacimiento* in their homes. Traditionally, a manger with Baby Jesus occupies the center, while Joseph, Mary, the shepherds, the wise men and some animals cluster around. The height of the figurines ranges from quite small to life-sized characters, while the construction varies with the use of cloth, cork, wood, paper, cardboard, or clay.

Some *nacimientos* are created with nine levels or steps. Every night, beginning on December 16 and ending on Christmas Eve, the figurines are moved up one level. In this way the Holy Family symbolically arrives at the manger at precisely the time many families are celebrating Christmas Eve. At times competitions focus attention and interest on the numerous and creative displays.

Posadas. Though the term literally means "inns," *posadas* are in reality a specific Christmas celebration in Mexico. The theme of this event is the search by Mary and Joseph for a place to stay during their trip to Bethlehem. The festivities surrounding this enactment continue for nine consecutive nights, beginning on December 16 and ending on Christmas Eve. Nine families usually participate, each family sponsoring one evening.

Each event begins around eight o'clock in the evening with songs and prayers. Then the company is randomly divided into two groups: one acting as Mary and Joseph and the other as the innkeepers. The groups walk slowly to a home while singing melodies such as *"¿Quién les da posada a estos peregrinos, que vienen cansados de andar los caminos?"* ("Who will give a place to stay to these pilgrims who are tired from walking the road?")

At the home, the "innkeepers" answer, *"Aquí no es mesón; ¡sigan adelante!"* ("There is no place here; keep on going!"). The door immediately closes and the group moves on. Then when the correct pre-designated residence is reached, those seeking shelter that evening are admitted to the "inn," and there is a great celebration.

During the first eight nights there are candies, fruits, nuts, and punch. On Christmas Eve the host family for that year supplies a large supper after a midnight mass, *la misa de gallo*, held at the local church.

The origin of the custom is said to be from an Aztec ceremony that a Spanish priest, Diego de Soria, adapted for Christian purposes. The continuance of this cultural tradition today contributes positively to a strong community life.

Las parrandas. *Las parrandas* or *trullas,* a version of Christmas caroling, are part of the Christmas celebration specific to the Caribbean area. Often beginning as early as the first week in December, the events sometimes continue until several days after Three Kings' Day.

In this activity a group of people, usually family and friends, go from house to house singing *aguinaldos*, traditional Christmas songs, accompanied by typical musical instruments such as guitar, maracas, güiro and timbales. After singing several songs, the group is invited into the home and offered something to eat and drink. Often an alcoholic beverage such as rum, beer or *ponche* (eggnog) is served, along with typical food of the season, which may be *pasteles, lechón, arroz con dulce,* or other tasty dishes. The group frequently continues singing and dancing for some time in the home before moving on to the next. Predetermined by group consent, the hosts of the last house to be visited treat their guests to hot *sopón* (thick chicken and rice stew), cooked while the singing and dancing continue.

The *parrandas* usually take place at night, and may even last until the next morning. They are also enjoyed during the day, on Sundays, Christmas Day, or Three Kings' Day. It is not uncommon for several neighboring houses to experience separate *parranda*s simultaneously.

The *parranda* is a beautiful tradition that unites people in the spirit of celebration. And the household that hosts the visit receives the gift of friendship in a spontaneous, colorful, and lively style.

SAINTS' DAYS

Each day of the Hispanic calendar is marked for one or more saints. When a newborn baby is named after a saint, that saint becomes that individual's *santo* and the particular saint's day becomes *el día del santo* for that person. To illustrate this, a little boy named Juan will throughout his life have June 24 as his *día del santo*; José will celebrate March 19; and Francisco, October 4; while a little girl named Guadalupe will celebrate December 12; Marta, February 26; and Catalina, April 29. For those celebrating this tradition, it is common practice to send cards and maybe even small gifts to friends on both their saint's day and their birthday. And even though this celebration has its roots in Catholicism, not all Catholics throughout the Hispanic world practice this custom.

LAS FIESTAS PATRONALES

Towns in the Hispanic world have one big celebration each year known as *las fiestas patronales* (Festival of the Patron Saint), a religious festival in honor of the town's patron saint. Although this *fiesta* has a Catholic origin, everyone freely participates in the festivities, even those living in remote areas surrounding the town.

The festival begins with a special mass held in the local Catholic church and continues for five to ten days. The main activities take place in the evening and include dancing, eating, fireworks, parades, shows, competitions such as the *paso fino* horses (horsemanship), and drinking—plenty of it.

One very popular event is *el palo encebado* (the greased tree). This activity requires a tall, straight tree such as a palm placed in the plaza; to its top are attached prizes, money, and meat, among other items. Groups of two or three persons attempt to climb to the top in order to grab one of the prizes. Adding greater challenge to this feat is the fact that the trunk has been thoroughly covered with automobile grease from top to bottom.

The *fiestas patronales* are eagerly anticipated by the town's youth, who use it as a time to make new friends and to become reacquainted with out-of-town acquaintances. These festivities are a memorable time for the entire town, providing a variety of typical events, music, food and fun.

11

Secular Holidays and Special Celebrations

It was a very special day in a school located in Barrio Pasto, a low-income rural community. Students were arriving dressed in their best clothes, ready for a day of festivities in honor of someone they considered very important in their lives: their teacher.

They entered my ninth-grade classroom with good humor, laughter, and spirits as colorful as their clothing. Today they were exempt from wearing the drab school uniform of khaki shirts and pants and black tie for the boys, and brown jumpers and tan blouses for the girls. As I looked over my classroom, I saw a wonderful mosaic of color and vitality. And why not? It was the celebrated *"Día del Maestro,"* which would end with an all-school dance.

For this special event through the years I taught in Puerto Rico, I received numerous gifts: ties, socks, cologne, and handkerchiefs. There were also the more innovative gifts of original poems or items personally created by students. The fact that some of my pupils were giving me the best of the little they themselves possessed was a significant gesture that surpassed the gift itself.

SECULAR HOLIDAYS

Besides the religious celebrations, a variety of secular holidays and special events are also enjoyed. The more common holidays include *Día de Año Nuevo* (New Year's Day), *Día de las Madres* (Mother's Day), *Día de la Bandera* (Flag Day), and *Día de la Raza* (Columbus Day). *Día de la Independencia* (Independence Day) is celebrated nationally according to the date when independence was acquired. In addition, each country has its own special days of celebration.

Vispera y Día de Año Nuevo

New Year's Eve is known as *la Víspera de Año Nuevo* and is celebrated with parties, dances, religious services or mass, plenty of food, and traditions specific to the country. In Spain, for example, twelve grapes are eaten by each participant at midnight with every grape representing a month of the year. The ritual is completed with the individual making a special request for the new year. Water is tossed out onto the street at midnight of the 31st of December in Cuba to symbolize good luck for the incoming year. Family gatherings and the formal giving of thanks for the past year of prosperity and family health describe the tradition in Mexico. And in Venezuela fireworks are followed by each participant eating twelve grapes in coordination with the twelve bells that ring out the arrival of midnight.

Día de la Raza

Probably the most widely celebrated secular holiday is *Día de la Raza*, known as Columbus Day in the United States. Observed on October 12, this holiday centers on the discovery of the New World by *Cristóbal Colón* (Christopher Columbus) in 1492, and is an occasion for parades and special programs recognizing the Hispanic heritage. *"Raza"* in this instance does not mean "race," but rather cultural unity. So on this day, the community of all people who speak the Spanish language is celebrated, whether they be white, Indian, or mestizo.

SPECIAL CELEBRATIONS

Among the normal working days are scattered special moments of celebration. Examples include *Día del Maestro* (Teacher's Day), *El*

Día de los Santos Inocentes (The Day of the Holy Innocents), and *el quinceañero* or *la fiesta de quince años.*

El Día de los Santos Inocentes

El Día de los Santos Inocentes (The Day of the Holy Innocents) has its origin in the religious event of King Herod's mandate to kill all children in order to eliminate the Messiah. Today it is a day full of fun in several Spanish-speaking countries, equivalent to April Fool's Day in the United States. In Spain and Puerto Rico, for example, it is celebrated on December 28 while in Mexico it takes place in November and is known as *El Día de las Mulas* (The Day of the Mules).

Pranks abound on this day. A university professor, for example, announces a surprise exam and then later indicates that it was done in jest. Or children are asked to run interesting errands such as to buy a hundred pesetas worth of glass. Even newspapers and radio stations participate in the spirit of the day. The tricks and the pranks played on these days are called *"inocentadas."*

Quinceañeros

A young woman's fifteenth birthday traditionally calls for a very special celebration known as *el quinceañero* or *la fiesta de quince años.* This important event, similar to a debutante ball or "coming out" party in some cultures, is most commonly celebrated in the Caribbean, Mexico, Central America, and Hispanic communities in the United States. Although the event is celebrated differently in various communities, there is frequently an elaborate fiesta to indicate this essential step in the life of the *quinceañera* (the fifteen-year-old): the threshold of womanhood. This time also often symbolizes the opportunity to begin wearing makeup, hosiery and high heels, and for some girls to commence to entertain potential suitors.

For families from the Roman Catholic faith, the *quinceañero* usually begins with a special mass given in the young woman's honor and attended by family and close friends. A fiesta then follows at her home featuring food, drink, conversation, and dancing. Traditionally, the *quinceañera* initiates this part of the celebration by requesting a dance with her father or another significant man in her family as her partner. After that, everyone joins in the dancing.

Fiesta activities may range from a modest family gathering to a gala social event in a rented hall. The customary party arrangements for the more wealthy families are often quite extravagant and elaborate. The *quinceañera* wears a special gown for the occasion and is accompanied by several of her closest female friends, dressed in identical gowns. Many times the same number of young men are also invited to be her *chambelanes* (attendants). The family sometimes hires an orchestra to provide the music, or rents a limousine or a horsedrawn carriage to transport the *quinceañera* and her attendants from the church to the place of the celebration. This very special event is often covered in the pages of the local newspaper, and at times is also announced on the local radio stations.

12

Sports, Pastimes, and Games

The ball was pitched and I hit a long fly over the fence. "Home run!" shouted the crowd, estimated at four people. Clad in a T-shirt and shorts on a February afternoon in Puerto Rico, I circled the bases with pride. When a call for supper interrupted the game, I went home and put away my homemade ball, which had been created by smashing a paper cup and covering it with masking tape. I washed up for supper, gently massaging my right hand, which was now feeling the effect of its use as the bat.

Playing ball on an empty lot was a favorite pastime for me as a child, but my compelling dream was to see a professional league game. Time after time I implored my busy father to take me, until finally after months of petitions, he announced that *mañana* we would go to San Juan to a game. That night I could hardly sleep!

The next afternoon, after several hours of traveling over curved and mountainous roads, my father and I entered the baseball stadium. The game was between two well-known rivals, and there in front of my eyes I saw some of my great heroes: Roberto Clemente, Orlando Cepeda, Rubén Gómez, Tite Arroyo. It was an unforgettable moment!

As I grew older, I went on to play Class B and Class A in my hometown, and during my undergraduate studies I participated on varsity teams in which teammates came from Puerto Rico, the United States, the Dominican Republic, St. Thomas,

Barbados, Trinidad-Tobago, Jamaica and many other Caribbean islands. This experience was rich and rewarding.

Needless to say, not everything was *"un mamey"* in this involvement, because pain was a companion. There was the time a ball from a hard-throwing pitcher hit me in the head; a day when my elbow stopped a lightning-hit line drive from just 60 feet away; another afternoon when my front teeth were knocked loose by the elbow of a runner sliding into second base; and the game in which I received a sore tailbone from a sizzling fastball. But it was all done for the love of the game!

SPORTS ACTIVITIES

Enthusiasm for sports is, without a doubt, an important characteristic of Hispanic culture, especially for men. Although practically all kinds of sports are enjoyed, the more popular ones include soccer, baseball, basketball, boxing, and cycling. Soccer, however, reigns supreme in almost all countries in the Hispanic world, except perhaps for Puerto Rico, Cuba, the Dominican Republic, and Venezuela where baseball dominates.

Fútbol americano (North American style of football), on the other hand, has received limited fan support. Wider transmission of sports events through television, the influence of North Americans residing in these areas, and the continuing interest of Hispanics returning to their country after having lived in North America, are possible contributing factors to its growing popularity in some countries. It is generally called *fútbol americano* to differentiate it from soccer, known simply as *fútbol*.

A reality of sports activities in this part of the world is the fact that there are very few women's teams, a situation that is slowly changing. For children and youth, too, sports competitions between schools are fairly infrequent. And for the adult who enjoys tennis and golf, access is generally limited to clubs and organizations, less often to the general population.

Soccer

As mentioned earlier, *el fútbol* or *balompié* (soccer) is the most popular sport. From the early age of two or three years, a little boy begins to explore the techniques of ball management under the tutelage of an enthusiastic parent—a very economical activity since the only equipment needed is a ball. Even if a ball is not available, one can be improvised out of paper or any other workable material. The game can be played practically anywhere: in the street, at the local school, in a park, on the beach, in a nearby field or in a vacant lot.

All Hispanic countries have a national soccer team. Every four years the international championship games, *La Copa Mundial* (the World Cup), are played. Teams from Argentina, Chile, Spain, Peru, and Brazil are especially famous. The enthusiasm for *La Copa Mundial* is phenomenal, reaching at times a level of fanaticism. During these games, life in the participating countries becomes practically paralyzed as the events are followed by radio and TV or actual attendance.

Baseball

El béisbol has its greatest fan support and involvement in the Caribbean countries. North Americans introduced the game to this region because its proximity to the continent and the ideal climate allowed for play year-round. Though it requires a bit more equipment than *fútbol*, baseball is still an economical sport, requiring only a ball, bat and glove, and an open space. With this sport, too, when the basic equipment is not available or financially accessible, children improvise: rubber balls, broom sticks and cloth gloves, for example. And with an enthusiastic parent introducing the game at an early age, a child often continues to play into adulthood.

The majority of the Caribbean countries have a professional baseball league and national teams, and many Caribbean baseball players are stars in the Major Leagues in the United States and Canada. *La Serie del Caribe* (The Caribbean Series) is an annual event with the participation of teams from Puerto Rico, Mexico, Venezuela, and Dominican Republic. The enthusiasm for these games runs high and the honor of being champion of this series is greatly valued.

Cockfights

La pelea de gallos (cockfighting) is a very old amusement commonly associated with the Hispanic world. In those towns that host the events, a building called *la gallera* is designed with a circular enclosure in the center. This eight to ten-foot enclosed area is the focus point of the fight, surrounded by raised seating where the fans congregate to watch and participate in the battle. It is sometimes said that the fight is more intense among the humans than among the cocks.

Bets—sometimes involving thousands of dollars—are placed on selected gamecocks. Usually held on Sunday, the fights begin in the morning and continue throughout the day, well past sundown. The number of events varies between ten and twenty per day.

In preparation for the event, sharpened spurs taken from other cocks are fastened with plastic over the spurs of the fighting cocks. These gutsy birds then fight gallantly and brutally until one or the other falls dead. At that time the bets are settled.

The level of noise in *las galleras* is remarkable—so much so that metaphorically to describe a very noisy situation or place the saying has evolved, *"Hay más ruido que en una gallera"* ("There is more noise here than in a *gallera*").

Bullfighting

For many Hispanics bullfighting is a form of art rather than a cruel sport. Considered as *el arte del toreo* (the art of bullfighting), it portrays the unique experience of a human confronting death. Even the famous American writer Ernest Hemingway said, "Bullfighting is the only art in which the artist is at risk of death." Yet, there is the reality of cruelty to the sport: Some 10,000 bulls are slaughtered in the ring each year.

The actual bullfight event, known as *la corrida de toros* or *la fiesta brava*, is divided into three parts. In the first, *los picadores* (lancers on horseback) injure the bull by jabbing the point of their lances into the bull's back muscles. Then *los banderilleros* stab *banderillas* (colorful sticks approximately 15 inches long) into the bull's neck muscles. In the third and final stage, *el matador* (killer of the bull) taunts the bull, using a cape in a display of bravery, artistry, and elegance. Finally, sensing *el momento de la verdad* (the moment of truth), *el matador* as the principal *torero* kills the enraged 1,000-pound bull by thrusting his sword between the animal's shoulder blades. A good *matador* kills the bull in the first attempt.

During *la corrida*, the audience shows excitement and pleasure through applause. As *el matador* accomplishes a successful *pase*, the onlookers at each pass of the cape will shout a rhythmic *"¡Olé!"* After the bull is conquered and killed, the audience waves handkerchiefs in appreciation of his successful work. Then as a token, *el matador* receives the ears, tail or hooves of the conquered bull, whereupon he walks around the arena showing his trophies to the spectators. This action takes place in a specific arena known as a bullring, *la plaza de toros.* A normal *corrida de toros* consists of a minimum of six bull-fighting events, sometimes more, each taking approximately twenty minutes per bull.

This sport, which traces its roots to the Roman circuses of the first century B.C., is popular and practiced in only a few countries, including Spain, Mexico, Peru, Colombia, and Venezuela.

Jai alai

Meaning "ball game" in Basque, *jai alai* is a unique Hispanic sport that is especially popular in Spain, Mexico, Cuba, and in the state of Florida in the United States. This game, similar to handball, is also called *pelota vasca* (Basque ball) or *pelota* (ball). It has its origins in the Basque provinces of northern Spain. It is played in a rectangular, three-walled court called a *frontón*, and is usually a competition be-tween two teams of one or two players each. The participants use a curve-shaped *cesta* (basket) to catch a very hard ball that is thrown against the wall. The principle of the game is basically that of handball, and the object is to bounce the ball off the front wall with such speed and spin that the opposition cannot return it before it has bounced twice on the floor thus losing the point. Because the ball can reach speeds of over 100 miles an hour, *jai alai* is considered one of the fastest and most skill-demanding sports in the world.

PASTIMES AND GAMES

Besides sports activities, the most popular pastimes in this culture are usually social. Conversing is a particularly enjoyable activity, whether in the plaza, on a street corner, on a porch of a residence, in a city park, or in a café while having something to drink. Going to the movies is also a fun way to enjoy oneself. During the weekends people visit relatives and friends, often eating together and conversing. These activities are simple, allowing people to connect and interact with each other in positive and enjoyable ways.

Popular Games

Many games that Hispanic children and adults play are also com-mon to other cultures. Common outdoor activities include jump rope, catch, hopscotch, and "Cops and Robbers," while board and table games such as puzzles, Chinese checkers, regular checkers, chess, cards, and dominos are often frequently played indoors.

Dominos is extremely popular among youth and adults and is played in practically any place: plazas, bars, porches, and beaches. Many times this game is accompanied by the consumption of alcoholic beverages such as beer or rum. Participants and spectators alike become involved in the lively conversation, and enthusiasm mounts as the game goes on. On occasions the game is played for money or for the next round of drinks.

Raffle and Bingo

For many centuries games of chance have been popular with both men and women, and are especially enjoyed in *fiestas patronales* and other public events. Since the raffle is a favorite way to raise money, clubs, schools, business firms, church groups, and even private individuals will raffle a cash prize or items of value or nostalgia. In addition, in towns of all sizes, weekend bingo games attract people of all ages.

Traditional Singing Games

Also influencing the social interaction of Hispanic children is a rich collection of traditional songs and games transmitted from one generation to the next. In spite of the growing attraction of television, computer and video games, children continue to cluster in the streets and school yards to play these singing games with their friends. As a rule the game is played in slow tempo, and the children skip or merely walk. Though the action is often the same, the words of the song may vary from one region to another. A Puerto Rican version of a popular Hispanic children's game is the following:

Yo soy la viudita,	I am the little widow,
la hija del rey,	The daughter of the King,
que quiero casarme	I want to marry
y no encuentro con quien;	I know not whom;
contigo, sí	With you, yes
contigo, no	With you, no
contigo, mi vida	With you, my dear
me casaré yo.	I will marry.

The children hold hands and form a circle and the group then sings and skips around the *viudita* who stands in the center. As the children sing "With you, yes," the *viudita* points to one child, and then to another when the group sings "With you, no." As they finish singing "With you, my dear, I will marry," the *viudita* grabs the hands of the first child and gently brings him/her into the center to become the next "little widow."

These singing games are usually learned from other children and are played spontaneously without adult supervision. Some of the games that originated in Spain centuries ago are still very much alive today.

La Piñata

Central to the activities of many parties for children is the breaking of the piñata. Made of tissue paper or cardboard, *la piñata* is a brightly colored item that has been shaped into the form of an animal, person, object or toy. Hidden inside is a clay jug filled with candies, coins, fruits, and other treats. The *piñata* is placed at the end of a string or stick, which is made long enough to be controlled by a designated person standing nearby. The children involved in the activity take turns being blindfolded and attempting to break the *piñata* with a strong stick or bat. When it is finally broken, the children jump upon the spilled contents with a great deal of enthusiasm and enjoyment, filling their pockets.

Specifically in Mexico, the *piñata* is part of each night of the Christmas *posadas*. And though it is usually associated with Mexico, the *piñata* is today enjoyed throughout the Hispanic world for any special celebration, whether a birthday party, baptism, or wedding.

13

Entertainment

The six of us met in the town plaza late at night to plan our activity. Our voices we had, but what we desperately needed was a guitar to accomplish our goal: to produce majestic sounds in the dark of the night for a romantic serenade to my sweetheart.

There in the plaza we pondered the problem of the missing guitar. Then Paquito, the only one among us who knew how to play, remembered that one of his good friends owned one. "Unfortunately though," Paquito lamented, "he is probably already sleeping." After debating which would be the greater challenge—a serenade without a guitar or a slumbering friend—we went after the desired instrument. We climbed the stairs to the second floor in a downtown apartment and went through several cycles of knocking and calling before the anticipated benefactor was awakened. An understanding youth, he lent us the essential instrument and we went on our way.

Some time later we were positioned outside the targeted window of a house in *el campo*. Inspired by the tropical stars above us in this Caribbean night, we began our concert of romantic songs—old and new. Though our eyes were fixed on the window, we saw no movement and the window remained closed. We strummed and sang some more. The window did not open. Now fear began to court our good intentions. We had heard too many nasty stories of unappreciative parents tossing out unwanted fluids onto unsuspecting serenaders, or even chasing them away with sharp and shiny machetes! Yet we continued, hope wavering. Wait! In the light of the Island moon, we detected movement inside. Yes, the window was opening and there was my girl, signaling her approval with a motion of her hand! Mission accomplished, we triumphantly headed back to town, invigorated with our success.

MUSIC AND DANCE

As the language of the soul and spirit, music and movement express the essence of the Hispanic culture. Through the generations, rhythms and patterns of movement have created *salsa, merengue, tango, chachachá, rumba, mambo, samba*, and *cumbia*. Contagious in their expression, the music and the dance have extended beyond Spain and Spanish America, a contribution to the world of arts.

Hispanic music and dance have been influenced by three main sources: the Spanish, the Indian, and the African. The guitar, mandolin, harp, *cuatro* (a ten-string instrument), and the *charango* (a stringed instrument made of an armadillo shell) show the Spanish impact. The Indian influence has provided the wind instruments, especially the flute. Finally, percussion instruments such as the drum, *congas*, and timbal have their origin in Africa.

The manner in which an area integrates or mixes the Spanish, Indian or African influences creates a vibrant convergence of unique regional expressions. The Caribbean is an illustration of how the rhythms brought by African slaves have inspired the Colombian cumbia, the Dominican merengue, and the Puerto Rican salsa.

Salsa

As the current red-hot and vibrant sound of Hispanic music, *salsa* is a good example to examine more in detail for its sound and dance combination. Contributing to its flavor are the elements of the more recent jazz, rhythm and blues, and rock, in combination with the Caribbean notes of Puerto Rican and Afro Cuban music. The sensorial *salsa* rhythms are filled with complex variations and the harmonies are unique in their richness. The best *salseros*, or *salsa* musicians, are genuinely innovative composers and interpreters.

Contributing Musicians

The Hispanic world has produced numerous musicians and singers who have achieved worldwide acclaim. In the area of classical music, examples include Andrés Segovia and Carlos Montoya as guitarists; Alicia de Larrocha, a pianist; and cellist Pablo Casals. Plácido Domingo, Monserrat Caballé, and José Carreras are famous operatic figures. Past and present popular singers include Julio Iglesias, Trini López, José Feliciano, Vicki Carr, Ritchie Valens, Gloria Estefan, Jon Secada, Juan Luis Guerra and Jerry Rivera, among others.

The more popular Hispanic-based music choices in the United States are the rhythmic salsa and merengue. Singers such as Olga Tañón (Puerto Rico), Oscar de León (Venezuela), Rubén Blades (Panama), and Juan Luis Guerra (Dominican Republic) are especially enjoyed by North American audiences.

Tunas

Accompanied by guitars or other instruments, the *tunas* are groups of students who sing together, at times receiving monetary compensation from bystanders for their performance. The *tunas*, or *estudiantinas* as they are known in some Spanish American countries, come from a tradition of the Middle Ages when many poor scholars needed to sing for their main meal. Even today, each school within a university generally has its own *tuna*, and occasionally the male students will stroll and sing through the streets at night, dressed in academic gowns while serenading their female friends. In response, the young women who are recipients of this pleasant attention, or the institution where the group has performed, frequently give ribbons to be pinned on the singers' robes as a token of their appreciation.

Mariachis

Originating in Guadalajara, Mexico, the *mariachis* are the brightly costumed strolling musicians who sing and play string instruments and trumpets. They play typical Mexican music, including the *ranchera* (a sad complaint of unrequited love), at fiestas, weddings, serenades, and other gatherings. Each musician dresses in a *charro* outfit, a Mexican cowboy apparel, complete with sombrero, waistcoat and fancy shirt, tight trousers with bells or floral decorations on the side, and boots.

The name *mariachi* is derived from the French word for wedding, *"mariage,"* and dates back to Emperor Maximilian's brief reign in Mexico in the nineteenth century. At that time, musicians were usually hired to entertain at marriage celebrations. Today mariachi bands are seen in other Latin American countries such as Puerto Rico and Costa Rica, for example, where they perform songs of the country in addition to traditional Mexican music.

Serenades

For many centuries *serenatas* have been the cultural expression of the romantic spirit of numerous young men. Late at night a group will get together to sing and play musical instruments, usually the guitar, in front of the window or porch of the young woman whose affection is desired by one of the group participants. If the young woman is equally attracted to her admirer, she will open the window to show her gratitude for the serenade. If, however, she is not interested or does not appreciate the event, the window or door will remain closed.

Serenatas are also performed for more serious relationships such as for a fiancee or spouse to accentuate the commitment and to publicly show the love between the couple. And in some communities it is a tradition for a young man to serenade his future bride on the night before the wedding day.

THE STAGE AND SCREEN

Within the Hispanic world the theatrical and movie traditions are strong. Most large cities have numerous theaters for plays, operas and variety shows, and many have hundreds of movie theaters. Mexico, Argentina, and Spain are important movie-making centers.

In addition, a good number of Hispanic actors and actresses have achieved worldwide recognition. Examples of these individuals include Ricardo Montalbán, Anthony Quinn, and Cantinflas from Mexico; Sarita Montiel from Spain; Fernando Lamas from Argentina; Rubén Blades from Panama; and José Ferrer, Rita Moreno, and Raúl Juliá from Puerto Rico.

Soap Operas

The global obsession of television viewers with the soap opera is shared by many in the Spanish-language part of the world. Here, many of the *telenovelas* are shown daily, while a few, due to their popularity, have become part of prime-time evening programming in some areas. Some *telenovelas* have continued for years.

The first Spanish American *telenovela*, *"El derecho de nacer"* ("The Birthright"), began in 1948 as a radio serial in Cuba with its first appearance on television in Mexico in the mid-1960s. Typical of many *telenovelas,* the theme of *"El derecho de nacer"* was of a protagonist searching for her true parents. One of the most successful *telenovelas,* though, was *"Simplemente María,"* created in Peru in the 1960s. Running for more than four hundred episodes, making it the longest running Spanish American soap opera, it developed the theme of upward mobility among the poor. *Telenovelas* in Spanish-speaking cultures usually focus on the trials and struggles of the rich and poor.

For many years *telenovelas* have mainly been produced in Mexico and Venezuela and exported to many countries, including the Spanish-language television networks in the United States. More recently, soap operas produced in Miami, Florida, are joining the market and are seen in a variety of countries, including El Salvador, Costa Rica, Venezuela, Bolivia and Peru.

Telenovelas are the most recent media offering, joining the already popular *radionovelas* and *fotonovelas. Radionovelas* can be heard on almost any radio station in the Hispanic world, while *fotonovelas* are sold in newsstands and local neighborhood stores.

14

Shopping, Economics, and Business

Down the steep and narrow street rolled the little cart pushed by a short man, his skin deeply tanned by the tropical sun. Cart and man moved along slowly together, both showing traits of many years of companionship, neither feeling a need to hurry. The cart was a mosaic of color, displaying along its edge tall slender bottles, partially filled with liquids in varying hues—an assortment of flavorings of *coco, piña, tamarindo*. Along the cart's once boldly painted sides was printed *P-I-R-A-G-U-A-S*; the man was known as *Mencio El Piragüero* to the people in my town.

That hot summery day with a coin in my pocket I was in search for a tasty and refreshing snow cone to satisfy my thirst. On Main Street just in front of the *Farmacia Moscoso*, I finally caught up with *Mencio El Piragüero*, tugged on his pants, and timidly asked for my favorite, a *piragua de coco*. Intent on each detail, I watched the old man scrape with deliberate strokes slivers of coolness from the huge chunk of ice, sparkling like a diamond in the center of his cart. Then just as calmly, he packed the crushed ice into a cone-shaped paper cup, and with the ease of one who has done this for decades, expertly poured on just the right amount of coconut syrup. Almost in synchronized movement, as *don Mencio* turned toward me, my little hand jerked from my pocket, nickel in hand. We made our transaction and I left, delightedly chewing on this special treat. Behind me, punctuating the busy sounds of the small Caribbean town, I could hear the "scrape-scrape" as *Mencio El Piragüero* did business with his next customer.

SHOPPING

The variety of shopping options in Hispanic communities includes small specialty stores, the local grocery store on the corner, the open-air and indoor markets, and street vendors. Other possibilities are the supermarkets and larger department stores, which are increasingly emerging in the larger cities.

Commercial hours vary from region to region. Generally, businesses open at nine in the morning, close for lunch from one until three, and then reopen until seven in the evening. Most are closed on Sundays and holidays.

A common occurrence upon entering most stores is the immediate and constant presence of a store employee for the duration of the stay. In fact, there may be more than one clerk, patiently standing nearby as a possible resource in the selection of goods. The fact that many employees work on commission and get a percentage of what they sell may account in part for this.

Bargaining is the mode of negotiation in some of these businesses. In others the goods have a set marked price.

In the smaller neighborhoods, *mercancía* (merchandise) can often be purchased *a crédito* (on credit). This is possible due to the friendly rapport between customer and the store owner, and their long-time acquaintance. The amount owed is written down in store records, and the customer pays later.

Peculiar to this economy as well is *la ñapa*, a term derived from the French word *"lagniappe."* *La ñapa* is an extra item included with a purchase. For example, when shopping for food, *la ñapa* may be one or two extra bananas, tomatoes or a couple of extra ounces of vegetables. Sometimes this gift is given spontaneously; at other times it is requested, especially if the customer has just made a significant purchase.

"Window shopping" with nothing specific in mind is not a frequent activity in this society. Customers usually go shopping with the purpose to buy something they need.

The Small Specialty Store

Even in communities where shopping options are varied, many people still prefer the social interaction of the smaller specialty shops. These stores cater to a specific line of goods and include *fruterías* (fruit shops), *carnicerías* (butcher stores), and *floristerías* (flower shops). Purchases are usually paid for in cash rather than by check or credit card.

The Neighborhood Grocery Store

Generally owned and operated by a family, this small store with its friendly and informal atmosphere becomes the place of reunion and connections for the neighborhood. *"Colmados"* in Puerto Rico and *"pulperías"* in Costa Rica are two of the names for these *barrio* (small neighborhood) stores.

Basic products such as soap, toothpaste, rice, beans, and milk can be found in the *colmado*s, and the merchandise is often sold in smaller quantities than in a supermarket. For example, it is possible in a neighborhood business to buy one egg instead of a whole dozen, or two cigarettes rather than the entire box. The items sold in these stores usually have fixed prices so the customer is not expected to bargain. Most people buy food at the *colmado* not only for its convenient location, but also because of the financial situation. Many families simply do not have enough money to buy in large quantities.

Open-Air and Indoor Markets

Mercados (markets) that are either open-air or indoors are very characteristic of the Hispanic community. The produce that is sold here is normally fresher and is sold more economically than in the supermarkets or in the small *colmado* or *pulpería.*

Generally the *mercados* are divided into several sections: one selling fruits and vegetables, and another fish and meats, while another concentrates on clothing. In larger cities crafts are sometimes included among the merchandise, and more recently, manufactured goods and technological equipment such as televisions and radios may be found.

Open-air markets are open on a specific day per week for business, while indoor markets are open on a regular basis. The most interesting time to visit these markets is on Saturday and Sunday when the area is full of action and shoppers. Frequently the prices are not fixed, so the customer is expected to bargain.

Some of the more internationally well-known open-air and enclosed markets are located in Mexico, Guatemala, and Peru.

Street Vendors

At practically any time during daylight hours and in almost every city and town, it is possible to buy a great variety of items without entering a store or market. This is done simply by approaching one of the many *vendedores ambulantes* (street vendors) who stroll through the neighborhoods or drive through the countryside selling their wares. The products offered for sale are varied: typical foods and drinks, vegetables and fruits, ice cream, freshly baked bread, clothing, personal accessories, household items, souvenirs, and more. This convenient way of shopping has been a traditional part of the Hispanic way of life for many generations.

One of the most picturesque of the street vendors is the person selling snow cones. Sold from a cart, the snow cones are called *piraguas, copos,* or *raspas,* depending upon the country. The vendor's cart is usually painted in vibrant colors, which, in combination with the assortment of glass bottles containing the flavorings, creates a vivid mosaic of color and delight.

Bargaining

The opportunity to *regatear* (bargain) gives an added flair to shopping. When bargaining, the merchant expects the customer to negotiate the given price and make an offer. A typical verbal exchange may take this form:

Customer:	*"¿Cuánto cuesta esta camisa?"* ("How much does this shirt cost?")
Vendor:	*"Cuesta treinta y cinco dólares."* ("It costs 35 dollars.")
Customer:	*"¿No la deja más barata?"* ("Would you give it for less?")
Vendor:	*"Se la dejo por veinticinco."* ("I will give it to you for twenty-five.")
Customer:	*"No, está muy cara todavía. Bájeme el precio un poco más."* ("No, it is still too expensive. Go down a bit more.")
Vendor:	*"Bien. Se la dejo por quince. No puedo bajarle más."* ("OK. I will give it to you for fifteen. I cannot go any lower.")
Customer:	*"Está bien. Me la llevo."* ("OK. I will take it.")

There are places, however, where bargaining is not appropriate. Generally speaking, bargaining is a normal transaction technique in the *mercado* but not in the shopping malls or in individual privately run stores. The attempt to bargain when it is not the mode of business risks giving a message that the customer is not happy with the quality of the product. To avoid making mistakes, it is best to observe native shoppers and follow their lead.

EMPLOYMENT

Historically in the Hispanic world manual labor has been undervalued. This attitude is especially prevalent among the middle to upper classes where manual work of any kind is avoided. Over time and by default, therefore, persons from the poorer class have done the work considered more degrading, domestic chores included. These workers generally earn very low wages and occupy the lower rungs of the social ladder.

Another characteristic of the employment situation is the hiring of several people to a task that could easily be handled by one. This is especially the case in public offices. In the Bureau of Motor Vehicles, for example, one employee revises a client's document, another signs it and gives the appropriate stamps, and a third takes the payment and provides the necessary duplicate copies. This job fragmentation, also seen in stores, on buses, in banks, and in the collection of garbage, stems from an insufficient number of jobs and an overabundance of workers.

Employment possibilities in this society also tend to be gender defined. More waiters are employed in restaurants than waitresses; bus and taxi drivers and bank tellers are generally men. Again, a probable result of job scarcity, this situation is compounded by the fact that since the husband is traditionally the main wage earner, available employment will go to him. Women, meanwhile, find work in the many domestic jobs available.

An additional characteristic of the employment reality is that young adults from the upper and middle classes usually do not join the work force while they are in school. Sometimes during vacation time, a son or daughter helps in a family business, but rarely is there employment at the blue-collar or manual level. Instead, the unmarried student continues to depend upon parental assistance until graduation.

For many employees, the job is considered an unavoidable part of human existence and only one aspect of life, so it does not always take precedence over other important personal activities. Thus, the resolution of a family issue may be perceived as more significant than presence at the job. This perspective governs greater flexibility for conversational interaction among employees while on the job, though not necessarily for all workers or employment places. Larger urban areas with industrial occupations, for example, have more rigid requirements, which ultimately affect expectations for employees.

CONNECTIONS

It is common in this economy to spend hours or days going from one public office to another in order to finalize a transaction. Whether an attempt to obtain an official signature, stamp, seal, or paperwork, the procedure is complicated, antiquated, and inefficient, and ultimately results in the loss of many hours of otherwise productive work time for the client.

However, there is a respected alternative that bypasses the system: the use of a *palanca* or *padrino*. This individual is often in a public position, is potentially available on a fee basis, knows the shortcuts of the procedures, and is usually known by the employees of the particular establishment. Often complicated and time-demanding proceedings become quite simple and uneventful—with the employment of a *palanca* or *padrino*.

Beyond the business context, the cultural need "to pull strings" and to have connections is very colorfully described by Spanish-language vocabulary and phraseology. *"Tener palas"* ("to have shovels"), *"tener un enchufe"* ("to have an electrical plug"), *"tener palancas"* ("to have levers"), and *"tener padrinos"* ("to have godparents") are all expressions illustrating the necessity for connections. This is further echoed by the well-known saying: *"El que no tiene padrino, no se bautiza"* ("He who does not have a godparent, does not get baptized"). Needless to say, there is an expected reciprocity in this system. Someone who has been a *pala* for another will expect equal assistance if the opportunity arises.

BRIBERY

Any discussion of monetary customs should include mention of the practice of bribery at the public level. Generally known as *el soborno,* and in Mexico as *la mordida* (literally "the bite"), bribery is widely accepted and commonly practiced. Government employees often earn extremely low salaries, so bribery has become an accepted way of enhancing income.

THE LOTTERY

The national lottery is very popular in most Hispanic countries, especially with those of lower income. Vendors selling *"los billetes"* (the tickets) are very accessible, setting up a table in the plaza or in shopping malls, or situating themselves prominently on main street, in front of the bank or a municipal building.

Every week participants part with a few coins, taking a chance at *el premio mayor* or *el premio gordo* (the grand prize). Some depend on luck while others seek a specific number that corresponds to their age, to the digits of a certain license number, to a dream they have experienced, or to the number they have consistently purchased week after week. A few individuals consult fortune tellers to learn their lucky number. At times when a cherished but expensive desire is voiced, a joking comment will also be added that the desire be fulfilled *"cuando me saque la lotería"* ("when I win the lottery").

THE PRESENCE OF BEGGARS

In towns, provincial cities and metropolitan centers, beggars are a common sight. Known as *limosneros* or *pordioseros* (literally meaning "For God's sake"), these persons can be seen asking for *una limosna* (a contribution) anywhere, but especially in the plaza, in front of churches, banks, or government buildings. Though many wear ragged clothes, others are dressed normally. Some will go from door to door in the residential areas asking for money. At times a small child will be sent to the house to make the request, since this holds potential for greater response.

The donor must practice caution in making the donation. A request for money to purchase food, for example, may ultimately be used to maintain a drinking habit. Longer residence in a community and better acquaintance with the residents of the area assist the donor in making wise decisions in giving.

Several factors contribute to the reality of begging as a way of life, including the high rate of unemployment, the favorable climate, and the big gap between the wealthy and the poor.

THE SALE OF USED ITEMS

In Spanish-speaking countries it is rare to see yard or garage sales. Instead, second-hand items such as stereos, computers, televisions, furniture, appliances, and books are usually advertised in the classified ad section of newspapers or in specialized magazines. Clothing and smaller household items are generally given away to family members, to the church, or to individuals who are less fortunate. People use an item until it is worn out or repair it until that is no longer possible, clear evidence of a society that does not practice a "throw-away" or "disposable" lifestyle.

CULTURAL VIEW ON MONEY

An abundance of terms, proverbs, and expressions in the Spanish language focus on the word "money" or express the value of money for the culture. *El dinero* is the formal term used for "money"; *la plata*, though more informal, is also used frequently. More colloquial or regional terms include *chavos* (Puerto Rico), *cheles* (Dominican Republic), *pisto* (Guatemala), *feria* or *lana* (Mexico), *billetes* (Chile), *pasta* (Colombia), *guano* (Cuba), and *reales* (Venezuela).

There are also a number of sayings in Spanish that relate to money. *"Estar navegando en oro"* is used to communicate that someone is "rolling in money." *"El tiempo es oro"* is the equivalent to the English expression "Time is money." And *"Poderoso caballero es don dinero"* (literally, "Sir Money is a powerful gentleman") parallels the English phrase "Money talks."

Proverbs dealing with money can reflect the values a culture holds important. Consider the traditional North American saying "A penny saved is a penny earned," which promotes the value of saving, of planning for the future, and of thoughtful expenditure of earnings. Equally revealing of the essence of Hispanic culture is the saying *"El dinero se ha hecho redondo para que ruede"* ("Money was made round so it can roll"), embodying the concept that money was made to be shared, to be spent, and to be enjoyed.

This flexibility toward the use of money is further evidenced in the repayment of very small cash amounts that have been borrowed, primarily by a friend or relative. Rather than paying back the borrowed money as soon as possible, there is the unexpressed understanding that "the favor" will eventually be returned, but not with money. To repay the exact amount risks communicating the message that the borrower believes the lender is very poor, badly in need of the money, or obviously stingy to be concerned about a few cents.

Many times this flexibility is also seen at the small business level when a few cents are involved. If the total for a purchased item comes to $5.05, for example, the typical store owner will often accept $5.00 and tell the customer "to forget" the rest.

15

Healthcare Alternatives

That afternoon at school I was not feeling well; my stomach was upset and my head was spinning. The five-mile curve-filled trip home by bus did not help my situation at all. Upon arriving at home I went directly to bed. My grandmother followed me to the bedroom and asked me what was wrong. *"Abuela,"* I told her, "my stomach and head hurt." Her brown eyes showed concern and her gentle hands touched my forehead, checking for fever. Immediately she assured me that everything would be fine and that I would be up and active in a short while. I trusted my grandmother. She was such a stable support for my whole family, and to me she seemed to know so much.

Abuela left the room saying she would bring me something to make me feel better, and sometime later, she came back with a herbal tea. She told me she had brewed this hot drink from *naranjo* leaves gathered in our backyard. Even though I did not like its flavor and harbored some doubts as to its effectiveness, I drank the whole cup. *Abuela* had made this extra effort for me, and after all, maybe it would help me to recuperate.

A few hours later I was feeling much better which seemed to please my grandmother. *"Nieto,"* she said to me, "my mother used that tea whenever I had a stomachache, and her mother used it too."

HOME REMEDIES

When illness strikes, products from the kitchen, backyard, or nearby field become the front-line approach in many Hispanic homes. The use of these items as home remedies is very practical since they are afford-able and accessible to many people. Many recipes utilized as home remedies have been passed down from one generation to the next, some of Indian or African origin.

The kitchen is the source for a number of home remedies. Garlic and onions, for example, are two food items that play a curative role in addition to their more routine culinary contribution. A clove or two of garlic is found to be effective in combating colds or diminishing a per-sistent headache. The onion, when cut and its odors inhaled, suppos-edly counteracts insomnia; or when sliced and rubbed against the scalp, it fights dandruff. And the ingredients for an easy-to-create tea to com-bat a cough can all be found in a kitchen cupboard: cloves, cinnamon and anise seed, sweetened with honey.

From the backyard or nearby field, *la sábila* (aloe vera) plant, which grows in abundance in some regions, is a home remedy used for the treatment of burns, small cuts and stomach problems. It is also used in the care and conditioning of skin and hair. And the basic ingredients for many medicinal teas used as home remedies are easily accessible out the back door. Examples of these teas are *té de manzanilla* (chamomile), *té de naranjo* (orange), or *flor de tilo* (linden flower).

CURANDEROS

The healing tradition of the *curanderos* (healers) has its roots in Indian and African cultures. In their practice, well-developed methods for treatment of illness include herbal medicine, exotic potions, or the evoking of supernatural powers through specific words or phrases. Even though the *curanderos* do not have an extensive academic back-ground, they are highly respected figures in their communities and are often preferred to trained physicians. The effectiveness of the herbal recipes and the wide range of knowledge acquired by the healer con-tribute to a respect by the community, a confidence not limited to re-mote areas, indigenous cultures, or individuals with limited education.

EXERCISE

Since walking and hard manual labor are a way of life naturally, "staying in shape" and special efforts at exercising are not made obsessively nor with any great intensity. This is changing somewhat in the larger cities, however, especially with the younger population. Gymnasiums and aerobic dance centers have recently been increasing in number in some metropolitan areas, and it is becoming more common to see people jogging or bicycling along streets or in city parks. The majority of the people, though, still manage to get plenty of exercise running errands or walking to work, to the bus stop, or to church.

THE PHARMACY

The *farmacia* (pharmacy) is usually a small specialized establishment offering medicines and personal care products. More recently in some areas, the larger chain-style drug store has also become available to the customer. When they become ill, the first step for many individuals is to consult the pharmacist. If the condition is serious, the pharmacist will recommend a visit to a physician, but for allergies, flu, colds, or minor illness, the pharmacist will often suggest an over-the-counter medicine. However, since the sale of medications in many of the communities is not strictly enforced, the local pharmacist may even suggest or sell an antibiotic, such as penicillin, without a doctor's prescription. At times the pharmacist will even write up a prescription, saving the customer a trip to the doctor's office. This practice is changing slowly as governments begin to regulate the sale of pharmaceutical products more strictly, but it is still common in many areas.

MEDICAL FACILITIES

El hospital, la clínica, el consultorio (doctor's office), and sometimes a home visit, are the options for medical care in the Hispanic world. The municipal hospital in many communities is a public health facility, subsidized by the government, and providing free or relatively inexpensive medical care. This helps to ensure that adequate medical treatment is available to all kinds of people, regardless of their income. The privately administered hospital in the same community may provide a broader range of services but for a more substantial fee.

Clinics are usually privately owned by a group of doctors. Treatment in this setting is often more expensive, but has the advantage of a closer doctor/patient relationship.

Doctors' offices are for out-patient treatment only. If a patient needs hospitalization, the doctor will make a referral to a *clínica* or *hospital*. Occasionally a doctor will make a house call in an emergency, but as ambulance services are becoming more available, this practice is decreasing.

16

Food and Drinks

It was a very popular place. As early as seven in the morning, there would be a line of people waiting in front of that old green building on *Calle Ruiz Belvis* in my hometown. The place was *La Panadería Las Delicias*; the product, crunchy elongated loaves of bread still warm from the oven. Customers liked it fresh and took it home to enjoy with *café con leche*, hot chocolate or juices. Whether it was breakfast, a mid-morning break, an afternoon snack following a long day of work and studies, or a bedtime filler, *el pan* from local *panaderías* was the context for refreshment, connections, and memories.

A tradition in my home occurred Sunday evenings after the services we attended at the church across the street. My mother would serve each of us a steaming cup of hot chocolate made from shredding a bar of *Chocolate Cortés*. Hidden in each cup, slowly melting, was a tiny chunk of the specialty cheese, *queso de bola holandés*. And heaped on a plate in the center of the table were buttered slices of *pan de agua* or *pan de manteca*. Bantering, serious discussions, and recollection of past events interwove our reality while chunk by chunk the plate emptied.

Years later I returned to the Island for my sabbatical, accompanied by my spouse and two sons. Living in a rural community a short distance from my hometown, we were still able to enjoy the warm crunchy loaves. While yet a distance from our mountainside home, we would hear the anticipated voice of the *panadería* employee over the loud speaker of his car as he went up and down side roads and around curves. *"Pan de agua,"* he would announce. *"Pan de manteca. Pan fresquecito."* Now he was at the foot of the steep incline leading to our community. Above the grind of his car motor, we could hear, *"Pan. Pan fresquecito."* Inside our house there would be a flurry of activity as we collected the needed coins, then out into the fresh Caribbean morning to the end of the driveway. "One loaf of *pan de agua*," we would request. Through the back window of his vehicle we could smell and see a multitude of tall white paper bags marching across the back space. Emerging from each bag was the toasted brown end of a loaf of bread, still warm. Loaf in hand we—another generation— would head back to the house, pinching off chunks and chewing as we went. The words, *"Pan. Pan caliente. Pan fresquecito,"* would drift back to us from the next curve.

VARIATIONS IN CUISINE

The cuisine in the Hispanic world offers a lot of variation, sometimes even within the same country. Dishes and their preparation style vary greatly from one region to another influenced by geography, weather and history. For example, in the Caribbean area *el plátano* (plantain), *el arroz* (rice), and *los frijoles* (beans) are basic; *el maíz* (corn) is central to Mexico and Central America; *la papa* (potato) dominates in the Andean region of South America; and the southern cone of South America enjoys an abundance of meat. Even the names used for a food item may vary according to the region; *frijoles, habichuelas* and *porotos* are all different ways of saying "beans."

Despite the variations, each area tends to have its specialty. *La paella* is a well-known rice dish of Spain that includes a varying assortment of chicken, sausage, seafood, and vegetables. *El arroz con pollo*, eaten especially in the Caribbean, is rice flavorfully cooked with chicken, tomato, olives and other condiments. *Las empanadas*, very popular in South America, are half-circle pastries filled with meat, cheese, or fruit. Enjoyed particularly in Argentina are *las parrilladas*, different types of meat prepared on the grill.

Historically Hispanic cuisine has been influenced by three main cultures: Indian, Spanish, and African. The Indian influence is shown in *las tortillas* (pancakes made from ground corn) of Central America and Mexico; in *los pasteles* and *las alcapurrias* (a mixture of grated roots, first steamed, then fried) of Puerto Rico; and in *las arepas* (a corn flour type of johnnycake) of Venezuela. The Spanish influence is noted in *el flan* (custard), *el café con leche* (coffee with milk), *el lechón asado* (roasted pig), and *el arroz con pollo* (rice with chicken). The custom of frying roots, vegetables or meat to accompany a meal reflects the African influence.

A visitor to this culture may be startled at the peculiarities of some of the regional typical foods: *morcilla* (sausage stuffed with spices, rice and blood), *lengua* (beef tongue), *modongo* or *menudo* (a stew of vegetables with chopped pork intestine), *chicharrones* (fried pork skin), *patas de cerdo* (pigs feet), or *patas de gallina* (chicken feet). Other dishes are unique in the manner in which they are served such as *pescado con cabeza* (fish served with the head still attached), and then there are the delicacies of the tail, the ears, and the feet of a roasted pig.

SPECIFIC FOOD AND BEVERAGE ITEMS

Without a doubt, each country could easily create several cookbooks detailing food preparation from its diverse communities. For the purposes of illustration, the following food and beverage items have been selected to be described in more detail.

Bread

El pan is a very important part of the daily diet in many areas. The typical loaf of bread of this area is similar in texture, appearance, and flavor to French bread. The loaf is long and features a thick, crunchy crust covering a chewy interior.

El pan is purchased fresh once or even twice a day directly from the *panadería* (bakery) or from street vendors, who transport their precious wares in simple carts. Residents in some rural areas receive service from vendors who travel in jeeps announcing their arrival over loudspeakers.

El pan, cut in thick slices, is especially eaten at breakfast, but is also enjoyed with other meals. It appears on the table in unique and interesting combinations: with ripe bananas, with avocado, with dried codfish and onions, with cheese, with *café con leche*, or with a cup of hot chocolate. Some loaves of warm, crunchy bread picked up fresh from the *panadería* never make it home!

The Plantain

El plátano is an appreciated complement to any meal, whether it is moderately ripe, abundantly ripe, or green. The usual technique of preparation for the ripe plantain is to first peel and then slice it horizontally, followed by pan frying. Overripe *plátanos* can best be prepared by baking in a moderate oven until the skins burst, a sign that the dish is ready for the table.

Meanwhile the green plantain, typical in a number of countries, is peeled, sliced diagonally, and fried until slightly tender. It is then smashed, refried, and salted, a tasty addition to regional dish combinations such as rice, beans, meat and salad. In this prepared form, green plantains are known as *tostones* is some countries; *patacones* in others.

Chili Peppers

Chiles or *ajíes* contribute zest to many dishes of the Hispanic cuisine. There are more than 2,000 types of chili peppers, many of which are cultivated in Latin America. They come in red, green, or yellow. Some of the most widely known peppers include the *jalapeño, serrano* and *caballero*.

The chili pepper is utilized in different ways: whole, sliced, minced, and ground. Though the *picante* (spicy) dishes of Mexico are most often associated with the chili pepper, many other Latin American countries have also experienced the culinary contribution of the *chile* or *ají* since pre-Colombian times.

The terms identifying the chili pepper show its cultural Indian connection. The word *chile* comes from the Aztec/Mayan *náhuatl* language, while the word *ají* has its roots in the language of the Caribbean *taíno*.

El cebiche

One of the unique dishes of Hispanic cuisine is *cebiche,* which is uncooked fish marinated in a mixture of lemon juice, hot peppers, and onion. Though there are several varieties of *cebiche*, a very popular combination consists of shrimp, cilantro, tomatoes, and onions.

Churros

A *churro* is a pastry especially enjoyed with coffee or hot chocolate for breakfast or a midday snack. Shaped into a cylindrical form, it is lightly sugared and crunchy on the outside, and sometimes has a pudding-like filling. *Churros* are sold in small shops or stands called *churrerías*.

Flan

A much-appreciated ending to a dinner is the sweet, light contribution of *el flan* or custard. As mentioned earlier, *flan* is a gift from the Spaniards to the current Hispanic cuisine. Though the most typical custard is vanilla, flavors also include *coco* (coconut), *calabaza* (pumpkin), or *piña* (pineapple).

Similar to other custards, the ingredients used to create this dessert are milk, eggs, flavoring, and sugar. In contrast to the others, a caramel syrup made from burnt sugar gives the *flan* a unique flavor and color. A recipe follows:

Flan (Vanilla)

—Preheat oven to 300 degrees Fahrenheit.
—Prepare caramel syrup by heating 1/2 cup white sugar over medium heat. Stir occasionally. When sugar is completely melted and has the color of very dark brown, pour into 13" x 9" cake pan or circular mold. The syrup will not completely cover the cake bottom at this stage, but will do so during the baking process.
—Into a blender container, add five eggs, one can condensed sweetened milk, one can evaporated milk, 1–1/3 cup regular milk, and one teaspoon vanilla. Mix vigorously. When completely blended, pour into the cake pan or mold.
—Bake in *baño de María* (hot water bath) for one hour. When cool, invert onto serving plate or cut into squares and invert individually when served. Makes 12–15 servings.

Coffee

Since approximately 1,000 A.D. when the Arabs learned to extract and boil it, coffee has been enjoyed. Today it is undoubtedly the most popular beverage in the Hispanic world. Coming from twenty-five kinds of coffee beans and consumed by one third of the world's population, it has also become the main export and income of many Spanish-speaking countries. Several of these countries are practically synonymous with well-known coffee: Colombia is one of the main world exporters; similarly, Costa Rica and Puerto Rico.

Usually served after the meal, coffee in this culture is much stronger in taste than the beverage ordinarily consumed in the United States.

Adults generally drink it strong and black in a demitasse to which sugar is added. This is known as *café prieto* or *café negro*.

Coffee is also drunk as *café con leche*, which is half coffee and half milk, served in a regular-sized cup and sweetened. In some areas school-aged children enjoy *café con leche* with their breakfast just like their parents, and at times even infants drink this flavored milk in their bottles. Bread or crackers often accompany *café con leche*, especially during mid-morning or afternoon breaks.

Mate

Mate is a tea drunk especially in Argentina, Uruguay, Paraguay, and in some parts of Chile. The container from which it is served, also called *mate*, is frequently a *pequeña calabaza* (a small dry gourd) or a pot of a similar shape. The *bombilla*, a special drinking straw, is used to sip the tea while the beverage is passed from person to person. To drink *mate* is a social activity, normally enjoyed with family members or a group of friends.

Piña colada

Especially popular in the Caribbean area, *piña colada* is also enjoyed in the United States and several Hispanic countries. Originating in Puerto Rico in the 1950s, the ingredients of the *piña colada* are typical of the island: cream of coconut, pineapple juice, crushed ice, and rum. A maraschino cherry often rests on top. Served "virgin" without the rum, the beverage is refreshing and delicious for all ages.

Ron and *Rompope*

Two popular alcoholic beverages in the Hispanic world are *ron* (rum) and *rompope* (eggnog). *El ron* is made from molasses, the residue remaining from sugar cane juice after the sugar has crystallized. Straight rum is more prevalent in the rum-producing countries such as Puerto Rico, Cuba, and the Dominican Republic. Elsewhere, rum is usually consumed in mixed drinks such as daiquiri, Rum Collins, piña colada, and *Cuba Libre*. Some internationally known rums from the Hispanic world include Bacardí, Don Q, and Bermúdez. Rum is also used as a flavoring in dessert sauces, pastries, and other dishes.

Rompope is a drink prepared with rum, milk, eggs, sugar and cinnamon. *"Rompope"* is the term used in Costa Rica, Ecuador, Honduras, and Mexico, though it may be named differently in other countries. In Puerto Rico, for example, it is known as *ponche* or *coquito*. *Rompope* is especially served during the Christmas season, and is often the expected treat during the *parrandas*.

17

Mealtimes and Customs

My mother would get up early every morning to prepare breakfast for my five siblings, my father and me. Since each of us would sit down to eat at different times, this caused a lot of activity in our household. Breakfast was simple, usually consisting of *café con leche,* bread or toast with butter, and juice. Sometimes my mother would stir up some oatmeal for those of us who liked it.

Since we children had a meal provided at the private school we attended, my mother would prepare a simple lunch for herself and my father. Rice, of course, was the staple ingredient. She would then cook some beans and fry some plantains to accompany it. Sometimes she would serve *bacalao con huevos,* a salted codfish and egg dish, or typical vegetables and roots with the rice.

For several years my mother worked during the day in a factory in town sewing gloves. Even during that time there was still an adult waiting for us when we returned from school, whether that was my *abuela* or a woman employed by my mother. As we trooped in boisterous from an activity-filled day, hunger was curbed with a cup of hot chocolate, *café con leche*, or juice and several slices of *pan de agua* or saltine crackers.

Our evening meal was served between five and six each day. My mother would usually prepare white rice and beans or a rice-meat combination. When meat was made as a separate dish, it was either stewed in a tomato sauce with seasonings, or fried. Salad consisted of lettuce with chunks of tomatoes and was flavored with a vinegar-oil dressing. *Mami* would call us to supper and then, from her position among the pots and pans in the kitchen, would individually hand each of us our filled plate. As dessert occasionally we would have candied fruits served with cheese or fresh fruits in season. My father would end his meal with a demitasse of strong black coffee, and as we grew older we would join him in both the coffee and the accompanying conversation.

My mother made it a habit to cook an extra amount since extended family members, customers of my father's business, *compadres* of my father, or family friends would oftentimes stop by. If the visitor did not care to eat, my parents would offer a cup of coffee. Extra food did not matter because whatever was left over could always go to Negi, our German Shepherd dog, or the two or three neighborhood cats that frequented our property.

MEALTIMES

The Hispanic culture counts three main mealtimes: *el desayuno* (breakfast), *el almuerzo* (dinner or lunch), and *la cena* (supper or dinner). In some countries morning and afternoon snack times called *la merienda* are also enjoyed.

Breakfast is eaten between six and eight o'clock in the morning, and is a very simple meal. Juice or milk, bread or tortillas, *café con leche*, a rice and beans mixture, eggs, prepared cereals or fresh fruits show the range of possibilities depending upon the region.

Traditionally, the main meal of the day has been *el almuerzo,* which is served between noon and three o'clock in the afternoon. After the meal, the adults often drink coffee and converse for a while, a custom known as *la sobremesa* (literally, "over table"). Recently, this pattern of the heavier midday meal has been significantly affected as more women are employed outside of the home and as irregular midday schedules in urban settings create time conflicts for family members.

Generally, supper is served after six o'clock in the evening, although in some countries such as Spain and Argentina, it is eaten between nine and ten o'clock at night. This meal is usually lighter than the midday meal. In those areas where lunch and supper are served at such a late hour, it is common to have a snack in the morning around eleven o'clock, and again about five in the afternoon. Often sandwiches or pastries are served at this time accompanied by *café con leche*, hot chocolate, tea, juice or a soft drink.

Some countries do differ from this pattern, however. Puerto Rico, for example, follows the custom of eating *el almuerzo* around noon. Supper then is the heavier meal served between five and six o'clock in the afternoon, and is referred to as either *la comida* or *la cena*.

In some areas, factory, agricultural, and other manual workers carry their lunches in *fiambreras*. This versatile carrier consists of a stack of four metallic pots fastened together with a wire cord, which serves also as the handle. Rice, for example, can go into one unit, beans in the second, and other meal items in the remaining pots, with the top unit covered by a lid.

AT THE TABLE

As in other societies, the Hispanic culture has accumulated its traditions for those moments together around the table. A sampling of some of these practices follow.

Seating Arrangements

In many homes, the chairs at the ends of the table are reserved for the parents. Guests in the home should feel free to sit along the side of the table, if another place is not indicated.

Use of Table Utensils

Most people follow the pattern of eating with the fork in the left hand and the knife in the right, maintaining this position throughout the main meal. During other times of the meal, the unused knife and fork rest on the plate with the handles on the table.

Passing the Food

Serving dishes, salad dressings, bread and butter are not routinely passed around the table, so it is appropriate to reach for and serve oneself those food items within reasonable distance.

Finishing the Meal

To indicate that one is finished eating, the used knife, fork, and spoon are placed across the middle of the plate. And since an empty plate indicates that the guest is still hungry, a bite or two left on the plate is a message to the hosts that satisfaction has been reached.

Interrupting a Meal in Process

"¡Buen provecho!" ("Enjoy your meal!") is the courteous phrase to use when entering a home or passing a group of acquaintances in a restaurant when a meal is in process. Should those at the table then give an invitation to join them around the table, they would likely say *"¿Usted(es) gusta(n)?"* ("Would you like to join me/us?"). The initial response to this invitation should be *"No, muchas gracias. ¡Buen provecho!"* or *"No, muchas gracias. ¡Que le(s) aproveche!"* ("No, thank you, enjoy your meal!"). However, if the group at the table persists in the invitation, it is appropriate to join them.

AT THE RESTAURANT

Upon entering a restaurant in a Hispanic neighborhood, a *mesero(a), mozo(a),* or *camarero(a)* (waiter, waitress) will generally greet the guests and escort them to an available table. Rarely is there a choice for a smoking or nonsmoking area.

Very likely, the individual serving the table is an older male. He will give each guest an individual menu, even though a display near most restaurant entrances also lists the possible dishes. Included on the display will be *el plato del día* (the special of the day). To order the meal, the verb phrase, *"Quiero"* or *"Deseo"* ("I would like") is generally used.

Near the end of the meal the waiter or waitress will offer coffee and dessert. In most places the bill is brought to the table only upon request by the guest, accomplished by catching the attention of the waiter or waitress and saying, *"La cuenta, por favor"* ("The bill, please"). Since some places include the tip in the bill, it is appropriate to clarify this with the waiter or the cashier.

Unlike other parts of the world, rarely are luncheons scheduled to "talk business." Instead, conversational topics tend to center around politics, sports, literature, economics, or family matters.

18

Clothing

It was during the 1950s when I was around eight years old that I first became aware of the *guayabera* shirt hanging in my father's wardrobe. It was long-sleeved and white with no decoration, so stiff with starch it appeared to have a shape of its own. Its simplicity in design and cotton fabric made it a very attractive and comfortable shirt for formal settings on a tropical island. My father, then in his forties, used the shirt for church activities on Sunday.

After some years, the *guayabera* hit a low in men's fashion and almost disappeared. I was in my twenties, already married with a son, and working as a director of a private school when it picked up in popularity again. This time, though, the *guayaberas* in my closet were of various colors with an assortment of intricately stitched designs. Cotton was still the main fabric, but combinations with linen and polyester had created a shirt that needed little or no ironing. I used the shirt to go to work, to church, and to any other dress-up occasion.

Now decades later, the *guayabera* continues to be a part of my wardrobe. I especially appreciate it during the hot summer days for a formal event when my only alternative would be a suit and tie. But an interesting development has occurred through these years. I no longer need to go to *Aibonito Elegante, La Tienda de Ginorio* or *La Ponceña* to buy a new guayabera. Even though I live in a medium-sized midwestern town in the United States, I can now purchase my *guayabera* shirts through the J.C. Penney catalog or occasionally in a Sears store.

CLOTHING STYLES AND APPEARANCE

In the Hispanic society significant value is placed on a neat appearance, especially in public. The culture's sense of pride, honor, and dignity translates into a societal norm of dressing nicely, though somewhat conservatively, both in style and color. The colors of black, gray, brown, and navy blue are often seen. Women generally wear skirts or dresses, although slacks and slacks combinations are becoming common in urban areas, especially among younger women. Men, meanwhile, usually wear dressy pants and shirt when out on the street. Though blue jeans and T-shirts displaying the names of North American universities are extremely popular among teenagers, casual or sloppy clothing is not commonly worn by the general public. For this culture, appearance and appropriateness of dress are more important than the cost of the clothing.

In many places children wear uniforms to school. A very common combination for boys is dark pants and a light-colored shirt with possibly even a tie; and for girls, a dark skirt or jumper with a light-colored blouse. All children wear dark shoes. Some schools have stricter expectations than others, such as not permitting girls to wear slacks or boys to wear jeans.

Occasionally in the countryside and in some villages, handmade, colorful, and elaborately stitched traditional garb can still be seen, particularly in those countries with larger Indian populations such as Guatemala, Peru, Bolivia, and Ecuador. In these communities the clothing is very similar to that worn by ancestors, with the style varying according to tribe, village, or region.

The amount of exposure to outside influences, primarily through the media, can affect the expectations of a community as to what is appropriate in apparel. For this reason, a traveler would do well to be sensitive to the host community's culture, and dress accordingly.

The *Guayabera* Shirt

As described in the introductory vignette, the *guayabera* is a typical shirt worn in Latin America, especially in the Caribbean area. This lightweight loose-fitting garment is made from a combination of materials such as cotton, linen, and ramie. Sometimes it is embroidered with bright, colorful and complicated designs, while at other times the embroidery design is simple, closely matching the color of the material. The shirt typically has patch-style pockets and is sewn with narrow vertical tucks running from top to bottom. It may have tiny buttons on each side near the hem.

The *guayabera* is ideal for the tropical climate since it is cool and fresh, yet dressy. It can be purchased with short or long sleeves. The long-sleeved shirt is considered to be more dressy and is often worn for formal occasions. The *guayabera* is never worn with a tie, and is not often seen with jeans or tennis shoes. The *guayabera* is most popular with men over thirty.

This simple yet attractive shirt, symbol of Latin America, has been worn through the years by politicians, executives, artists, and individuals both prominent and common. The famous Latin American writer Gabriel García Márquez, for example, was wearing a *guayabera* when he received the Nobel Prize for Literature in 1982.

Short Pants

The use of short pants is not as common in Hispanic countries as it is in the United States. In many communities, shorts are worn at places of recreation such as the beach or at home, but not in public places like classrooms, church, or work settings. In fact, in some public offices, entrance is not permitted to people wearing shorts, and in some areas the use of shorts is so much considered a characteristic of tourists, that any resident who appears wearing shorts runs the risk of being ridiculed as a *turista*. In some instances the disapproval is so strong as to produce a reaction of verbal and/or physical harassment.

On the other hand, shorts for both men or women are accepted garb in some other areas of the Hispanic world. Exposure to outside trends influences this flexibility. The geographical location also contributes to the acceptance and perception of the use of shorts. For example, a city on the coast in a warmer climate may be more tolerant than a metropolitan community in the mountains.

SIZES OF CLOTHING AND SHOES

Shoppers buying clothing items in Spain and Latin America will look for different-size numbers than their friends and relatives in the United States. The following examples show these differences:

Item	U.S. Size	Spain/Latin America Size
Dress	12	40
Pantyhose	9	2
Shoes (women)	8.5	39
Suit (men)	42	52
Shirt (men)	16	41
Shoes (men)	8	40

19

City and Town Settings and Ambiance

The time was Saturday evening and I was going out. I had put on my best clothes and my hair was combed to perfection. It was a weekend tradition for me, along with the other young people in my town. The center of action, conversation, and promenade was la plaza, a meeting place where I could spend hours talking to my male friends and could watch the young women from our town walk by in pairs or in groups of threes or fours. Located in the hub of town, our plaza in Aibonito was surrounded by the Catholic church and several main businesses and public offices, and was attractively landscaped with trees, tropical bushes, and flowering plants.

This Saturday night my friends Cuco, Víctor, Paquito and Feliciano had already arrived at our usual meeting spot: the bench beside *El Kiosko de Don Juan*, where don Juan sold his famous *piña* and *coco* candy. The discussion of the evening commenced with the general theme of baseball and gradually narrowed to the dubious question of who was a better player, Mickey Mantle or Willie Mays; Roberto Clemente or Peruchín Cepeda. Then we moved on to the political situation of the Island. This was an election year and as usual there were interesting candidates for the political parties supporting statehood, continued commonwealth status with the United States, or independence for the Island.

While we were talking, laughing, arguing, and gesticulating, we were also visually taking in the other action in the plaza. Among the pairs and groups of peers walking slowly past our bench was a very attractive young woman. She was a brunette with long hair cascading down her back, and I noticed that her dark eyes had caught mine several times during the evening. I wanted to see her go by at least one more time, but it was already eleven and I had to go home. That was OK, though, because there was always next Saturday at the same time in the same place, the plaza.

THE METROPOLITAN AREA

Metropolitan areas in the Hispanic world are generally conservative in the use of space. Residential lots are small, and even neighborhoods possessing more yard area usually do not waste a great deal of space on lawns and gardens.

Even though the center of the larger cities have older homes, at times quite dilapidated, the poorer sectors are found on the outskirts. These *arrabales, villas miserias,* or *barriadas* (slums, ghettos) are frequently constructed out of tin and cardboard. Their occupants are often *campesinos* (peasants) who have migrated to the city in search of work or a new life. All too often they discover that the new home is even less satisfactory than the life they have left in *el campo*. Into their reality come disorientation and alienation: The city is big, life is full of stress, the noise is bothersome, and unemployment is almost inevitable.

Meanwhile for those who are in the middle or upper classes, the urban experience is distinct. Living in sectors of the city, known as the *barrios, colonias* or *urbanizaciones*, these residents often experience a style of life with basic necessities and luxuries provided. Thus, contrasts abound in the metropolitan area: In the main plaza a child is sleeping on a piece of cardboard while a BMW or Mercedez Benz drives by.

Architecturally the urban areas display yet another set of contrasts: The contemporary and the old exist side by side. A modern skyscraper, for example, is constructed right beside a sixteenth-century building, illustrating the aura of this culture that values the glory of the past, yet embraces the progress of the future.

Cities share many similarities with each other in physical layout, style of life, order of business, transportation, and expectations of safety and well-being. Each city, however, has its own unique characteristics.

Ethnic composition varies, as does architecture, and some cities are older than others. Climate contributes to different rhythms of life and general ambiance, too. Geographical location affects metropolitan personality depending on whether the city is located in the interior of the country, in a mountainous region, or on the coast. And a large urban center is different from a medium-sized city in one of the surrounding provinces.

The impact of transculturation is a reality in many major metropolitan areas today. For the Spanish-American region, the influence of the United States is quite noticeable, not only at the political and economical levels, but also in culture, values, attitudes, beliefs and life style. Media commercials in these areas advertise many North American products, and franchises such as Sears, Burger King, McDonald's, Pizza Hut, Denny's and Kentucky Fried Chicken are part of the urban scenery in many metropolitan areas.

THE PLAZA

On the average weekday the streets of a small town or village are vibrant with a great diversity of colors, sounds, smells, and activities, involving all ages and social classes. At the heart and center of the action is the plaza, planted with flowers and shrubs, and often decorated with fountains and monuments of military or literary heroes. Most plazas are crisscrossed by paths featuring benches where people sit to chat, read, play dominoes, or feed the pigeons. Displayed on some of these benches is an inscription of the donor or the bold advertisement of a product or local business. Important buildings surround the plaza, often including the main church, banks, the post office, municipal offices, the courthouse and some shops. Street vendors set up their carts or kiosks in or near the plaza, taking advantage of the greater level of pedestrian traffic.

In small towns the plaza is also the location for the celebration of municipal festivities such as *fiestas patronales* or political meetings. And for many youth, the plaza is the ideal spot to meet and talk with friends and to watch members of the opposite sex go by.

STREET ADDRESSES

Most addresses in cities and towns are written with the name of the street first, followed by the number of the house or building. For example, correspondence sent to a residence at 1714 Mango Street would be addressed to *La Calle Mango, número 1714,* or could be shortened to *Mango, 1714.* On occasion, if the house number is mentioned first, it is stated as *El 1714 de la Calle Mango.*

Numbers within addresses, as well as telephone numbers, are generally grouped into sets of two when given orally. Thus, the residence at 1714 Mango Street is located at *número diecisiete catorce,* not *mil setecientos catorce.*

In some places a system other than specific street names and numbers is utilized. Directions in Costa Rica, for instance, are given by distances in meters using a landmark as a reference point. Thus, a taxi driver given the address of a residence *300 metros norte, 150 este, de la Iglesia Santa Teresita* (300 meters north, 150 east from the Santa Teresita Church) would locate the house without difficulty. Yet the same taxi driver would likely have more difficulty arriving at the same location were the instructions given by the street address and house number.

20

Building Construction and Lodging Arrangements

Concrete posts and foundation provided the base for the five-foot cyclone fence that surrounded our home in a small town in the mountainous interior of Puerto Rico. Closing off the driveway was a cyclone-fence gate. When a stranger came on business or to request information, the person would wait and call from the gate, *"Señora. Señora."* My mother then either invited the visitor to the house or went out and talked to the caller through the closed gate.

Our house did not have iron latticework over the windows, porches and entrance areas, although many homes on the Island did. The purpose for the strong fences and metallic latticework went beyond Spanish influence for home design; it was for protection.

In traveling to other Latin American countries, I was able to see yet another style of property safeguard. On one occasion, having arrived the night before to a friend's home, I woke up the next day and looked out the back windows facing his patio. Surrounding the entire area was a tall concrete fence topped by a jagged multicolored edging. Out of curiosity I asked my friend about his patio fence. He explained that broken bottles had been cemented into the fence during its construction for the sake of security. This is a common practice in his area, he commented, as well as in other Latin American countries.

HOME DESIGN AND CONSTRUCTION

Though it is difficult to make a general description of houses in the Hispanic world, there are some typical features. Houses tend to be small and close together. Windows and even entire house entrances are frequently covered by attractively designed *rejas* (iron latticework). Very often tall brick or stucco walls surround the house and its tiny yard. An entrance gate then provides access to the property, requiring visitors to ring a bell or to call out and wait for the invitation to enter. Many times several families share the same gate or entrance way.

While some houses have inner patios with adequate space for a garden, plants, a fountain, or small sculptures, many more homes have only a small back patio. In this walled-in area children play; laundry is aired; fruits, vegetables, and herbs are grown; pets have their homes; a hammock is hung; and many other activities occur.

Homes are frequently built with flat roofs. Many times these are put to good use as an area for washing the clothes or hanging the laundry to dry. Sometimes an additional room or an entire house is constructed upstairs for a maid or relative.

In some small towns and rural areas modern conveniences are almost nonexistent, or a home may have only cold running water

Wall-to-wall carpeting is rare. More often the floors are either of highly polished wood or of *baldosas* (glazed ceramic floor tiles). These tiles, also known as *losas*, have solid colors or designs which, arranged together, may form a larger pattern. The walls of many bathrooms and kitchens are covered with *azulejos* or glazed ceramic wall tiles.

In place of built-in or recessed closets, many homes use *armarios* (armoires) or *roperos* (wardrobes) to hang clothing and to store other personal items.

MULTILEVEL BUILDINGS

The terminology used in Spanish to define the different stories or floors of buildings can cause confusion to the English speaker. The basement is called *el sótano*. The first floor is known as *la planta baja* rather than the expected *"el primer piso."* So the next floor, designated as the second story in English, becomes *el primer piso* for the Spanish speaker. The following charts this out:

Basement	Sótano
First floor	Planta baja
Second floor	Primer piso

| Third floor | Segundo piso |
| Fourth floor | Tercer piso |

In some apartment buildings the thirteenth floor is omitted in deference to those who feel the number "13" is symbolic of bad luck, tragedy, or disaster.

HOTELS, INNS, AND ROOMING HOUSES

Visitors traveling in the Hispanic world have a choice of several lodging options. Metropolitan centers usually have conventional hotels, fluctuating from the five-star to the small hotel in a more remote area. The larger hotels likely offer more comfortable or even luxurious facilities such as swimming pools, air conditioning, hot water, spas, or restaurants and bars with nightly entertainment.

Travelers can also obtain lodging and meals at smaller establishments or inns known in different countries as *mesones, hostales, fondas,* or *posadas.* In these, sometimes, guests are expected to bring their own sheets and towels for their personal use.

Pensiones or rooming houses are also an economical option. Since a *pensión* often occupies a section of the owner's home, it is typically small and quite simple, yet comfortable. Characteristically it has an informal and family atmosphere. *La pensión* is ideal for families or individuals interested in economical lodging since lunch and supper are often included in the price. Guests can spend several days or remain longer. Students living abroad, for example, sometimes rent a room in a *pensión* for a semester or for the entire year.

21

Transportation

On weekdays and Saturdays the main street in my hometown was packed with action. Buses, trucks, cars, motorcycles, and bicycles all competed for access. Pedestrians further complicated the flow of traffic through the narrow streets. In practice, there seemed to be an understood hierarchy regarding right-of-way, with buses and trucks heading the order of importance, followed by cars, then motorcycles, bicycles, and last of all pedestrians.

A discordant symphony of sounds accompanied this activity: accelerating motors; squeaking brakes; human shouts and greetings; and the ever present, all-powerful horn. In my town and elsewhere, it was through the horn that greetings were sent, warnings expressed, and frustration vented. In that split second when the red light was changing to green, horns were already indicating that traffic should be moving. Defensive and offensive driving were possible, thanks to the handy and much-utilized horn.

Oddly enough, despite the madness there was a courtesy to this flow and noise of traffic. On a busy afternoon one weekday, my little sister accompanied me downtown to *El Colmado Carrasquillo* to pick up a quart of milk and some tomatoes for supper. Since our home was only about 300 meters from the main thoroughfare through town, it did not take us long to walk to the principal intersection. However, it did seem to take forever until we had sufficient space between vehicles to cross. Holding hands we started out hesitantly, when a suddenly appearing car announced its approach with a loud blare of a horn. Startled, my sister practically jumped up on my back. Then a very courteous and thoughtful event occurred: Amidst that confusion of downtown activity, all traffic came to a complete stop, purposely allowing my little sister and me to safely cross the street.

TRANSPORTATION OPTIONS

Due to the economical and geographical realities of many of the Hispanic countries, private ownership of vehicles is limited. Most residents living in these areas depend instead upon public transportation systems, which provide numerous and varied options within and between cities. Their inexpensive and extensive services are accessible to persons from all social levels.

The Automobile

The automobile with all its advantages and disadvantages is a growing presence in many of the Hispanic countries. Those who are financially able to own a car will generally possess a smaller model. This is because the vehicle itself and its parts are expensive, fuel costs tend to be high, and larger cars have more difficulty maneuvering the many steep and narrow roads. In addition, parking is scarce and expensive.

The Motorcycle

Motos (motorcycles) are a more affordable and thus common means of transportation, especially within the cities. Very typical is the use of the tiny "moped" model, which is hardly bigger than a bicycle. Larger more luxurious motorcycles are very rare.

Taxis

Taxis come in a variety of colors and models. Their service is accessed by a phone call or, if on the street, by waving down an available vehicle. Due to the unstable inflation rates in some countries, not all drivers use the meter system to determine the service fee; so generally the passenger asks about the price, and sometimes needs to agree on a rate before taking the taxi. Once at the destination, it is customary to give the driver a good tip.

The Bus System

Because of its extensive route layout, the bus system is the popular choice of public transportation options. Routes incorporate frequent stops, allowing passengers to board or exit. Normally, people wait for the buses at a designated *parada* (bus stop), but in some areas a bus can be flagged down along the road or street.

For longer trips between cities, passengers are required to purchase tickets to reserve a seat. Luxury buses are often equipped with restroom facilities, and at times a meal in transit is included in the price of the ticket. Often another person will accompany the driver in order to collect the money or tickets as the passengers enter the bus. In some cities smaller vehicles called *microbuses* combine the function of a bus and taxi: shorter routes, fewer passengers, and a fixed fare.

While buses vary from one system to another, ranging all the way from modern to older models, each bus assumes its own personality by virtue of its flamboyant colors, decorations, or boldly displayed name. Bright red or dark green, with colorful designs, are common colors. The national flag or religious pictures frequently decorate the interior. Many times painted onto the exterior side might be the name of the bus: *"Mil amores"* ("A Thousand Loves"), *"La Maravillosa"* ("The Marvelous One"), or *"La Orgullosa"* ("The Proud One").

On bus routes in more remote areas, it is not uncommon for human passengers to share space with animals. Chickens, dogs, or even goats accompany their owners to desired destinations.

The Subway System

Any stereotypical image of the Hispanic transportation system consisting of dilapidated taxis and of antique buses packed with passengers hanging out of the doors and windows is strongly challenged by *el metro* (the subway). *El metro* is one of the public transportation options available in some of the larger cities such as Madrid, Barcelona, Mexico City, and Buenos Aires. These systems are quite extensive, sophisticated, and heavily utilized. The Mexico City metro, for example, consists of 136 kilometers of track and 105 stations. More than four million people ride this subway system daily.

THE HORN

As mentioned in the introductory vignette, in this culture a vehicle's horn is often used. When picking up friends at a home, sounding the horn gives notice that the driver has arrived and is waiting. When a friend is seen among the pedestrians on the sidewalk or among the vehicular flow, a tap of the horn says "hello." When traffic does not flow easily, drivers blow their horns to show dissatisfaction. When a driver negotiates a series of blind curves, the horn communicates a warning to approaching traffic. And sometimes a tap of the horn even substitutes for the act of stopping at an intersection. Because they use horns so regularly, vehicle owners sometimes enjoy creating new sounds for their instruments; besides the traditional honks and beeps can be heard whistles, tonal phrases, and segments of tunes.

THE HITCHHIKER

Hitchhiking is a rare activity in Spanish-speaking countries. In fact, standing by the road, thumb in position, asking a ride from a unknown driver does not meet cultural approval. Besides negatively classifying the person, hitchhiking is also considered dangerous. If a person still feels that hitchhiking is necessary, it is more tolerable to a community if the traveler is male. The expectation is that if free transportation is needed, friends, relatives, or a neighbor are more than willing to lend a hand. In addition, the relatively inexpensive public transportation—the bus system, for example—diminishes the need to hitchhike.

The hitchhiking terms describing "to ask for a ride or lift" are colorful in Spanish and vary from one country to another, as illustrated in the following list that includes literal translations:

Spain	*hacer autostop*	(to make an auto stop)
Peru	*tirar dedo*	(to toss the thumb)
Panama	*pedir o dar un bote*	(to ask for or to give a boat)
Nicaragua	*pedir un rai*	(to ask for a "ride")
Venezuela	*pedir la cola*	(to ask for the tail)
Guatemala	*pedir un jalón*	(to ask for a pull)
Mexico	*pedir un aventón*	(to ask for a push by a strong gust of wind)
Cuba	*pedir botella*	(to ask for a bottle)
Puerto Rico	*pedir pon*	(to ask to be put in a place)

22

Communications

I finished eating my supper in a rush and left running to my neighbor's house. Already seven or eight persons were standing in the doorway, while Sr. Brito and his family were sitting comfortably inside on the chairs and sofas of their living room. Effortlessly I manipulated my slender body around the adults in the doorway, and found myself a center-front position. Unfolding before my eyes in black and white were the entertaining episodes of *"Cisco y Pancho,"* sponsored by *La Leche Pet*, on the only television in town.

With the program over I walked slowly home, mulling over in my mind a persuasive approach to convincing my parents of the advantages of owning our own TV. It seemed to me that one strong argument in favor of such possibility would be that I, their eldest son, would no longer need to go to a neighbor's house at night.

My father must have agreed with me because some time later, on returning home from school one day, my grandmother greeted me with the news that a television had just arrived. She further informed me that a tall pipe with wires, called an antenna, had been attached to the roof of the house for the purpose of reception. This last bit of information triggered my innocent curiosity and I determined to climb up onto the flat roof of our home to check out that phenomenon. Out back of our house I found the pipe that ran up the height of the building, and with an impressive jump I was soon on my way, hand

over hand. Almost to the top I encountered an obstacle that
significantly discouraged my exploration into the wonders of
that technology: a direct confrontation with the angry tenants
of a wasp nest. It became one of the ironies of my life that
with my eyes subsequently swollen shut, I was unable for several days to enjoy the new television for which I had worked
so hard.

TELECOMMUNICATIONS

Especially in the larger cities technology has made a major impact on
the Hispanic world. Many homes have the electronic conveniences of
computers, cordless telephones, electronic games, or video cassette
recorders. As these products continue to increase in use, they will undoubtedly affect the style of life in many communities. Indeed, im-
ported technology has already made its impact upon the Spanish language. Along with the arrival of the equipment comes new technical
terminology. Many times the new terms are accepted and modified, as
has happened with the computer phrase "to format," for example.
Adapted into Spanish, it has become *"formatear."* Other times, a word
or phrase may be adopted without changes, as has occurred with the
term *"software."*

Television

Television has completely entered the Hispanic world, becoming at
times the main source of entertainment. Each country has its own news,
music, comedy and soap operas. Contributing significantly to TV entertainment is programming coming from the United States, translated into
Spanish. Translated North American programs that are currently most
popular in Hispanic America include "Baywatch," "Oprah Winfrey,"
"Hill Street Blues," "MASH," and "The Cosby Show."

Conversely, Spanish-language television is seen both in larger North
American cities such as Chicago, New York, Los Angeles and Miami,
and in Hispanic communities throughout the country. At this time, the
more frequently subscribed networks in Spanish within North American
are Univisión, Galavisión, and Telemundo, while *"Sábado Gigante"*
with Don Francisco (Mario Kreutzberger) is a Spanish-language favorite. Seemingly capturing the essence of what is considered good television and entertainment, *"Sábado Gigante"* is produced in Miami and

is seen by more than 40 million people Saturday after Saturday in the United States and Latin America.

Telephone

Even though each year more phones are being installed, there are still some communities where homes do not have service and some neighborhoods without access to a public phone booth. In many areas a strong bureaucratic system tends to bog down the process for acquiring the service. In addition, the expense involved in setting up the equipment, purchasing the phone, and maintaining service all contribute to create lengthy and delayed installment and maintenance.

The advent of the cellular phone has revolutionized telephone communication and has created broader accessibility. In some communities this portable communication device seems to be everywhere: at the beach, in the shopping mall, on the street, in the car. Some users combine the technology of the cellular phone with that of the individual beeper, not only facilitating communication and cutting costs but also serving as status symbols.

Public Phone Use. When it is necessary to make a long distance call using a public telephone, the procedure must be learned, since it varies from one area to another. In one locality, a caller must go to a main or branch telephone office where a booth is assigned and the call is placed by an operator. Immediately upon concluding the call, payment is made. In other settings, *fichas* or metal tokens are use to operate the public telephone. The *fichas* are acquired at the local telephone office or at a neighborhood business. Yet another arrangement is the use of phone cards.

Procedural Phraseology. The manner in which the telephone is answered in Spanish also differs from country to country. *"¡Hola!," "¡Aló!," "¡Diga!," "¡Dígame!," "¡Bueno!," "¡Oigo!,"* and *"¿Qué hay?"* are some of the common ways. Occasionally one of these phrases will be followed by the family name, *"¡Hola! Familia Meléndez."* Meanwhile, a company or small business may receive a phone call with the words, *"A la orden"* ("May I help you?"). Callers usually then identify themselves by saying, *"Soy María Hernández"* or *"Habla María Hernández"* ("This is María Hernández speaking"). If the caller wishes to speak with someone other than the person answering the phone, this can be done formally, *"¿Me puede comunicar con Elena?,"* or informally, *"¿Está por ahí José?"* The response "May I ask who is calling?" has its equivalent in Spanish in *"¿De parte de quién?"* and can be answered *"De parte de Pablo"* ("Pablo is calling"). If the one who answers the phone is also the person requested, the reply *"El/Ella habla"* or *"Un(a) servidor(a)"* equates with the English "I am s/he" or "Speaking."

Numerical and Alphabetization Patterns. Telephone numbers in some Hispanic countries are arranged in seven digits (716–2834), while in others a pattern of six is used (48–16–92). When telephone numbers are given verbally, they are spoken in sets of two. For example, a number of 534–8466 would be given as *"el cinco treinta y cuatro, ochenta y cuatro, sesenta y seis."*

In the phone directories, names are alphabetized by the first last name (the paternal). The entry next includes the second last name (the maternal) and ends with the given first name. Since there may be several individuals with the same first and last names, it is important to know both the paternal and maternal last names.

WRITTEN COMMUNICATION

Information and news spread, verbally or in writing, in the Hispanic community whether in a small rural *barrio* or the bustling metropolis. Small towns usually do not have a local newspaper. Newspapers purchased on the street or delivered to the home are generally created in and distributed from a larger city. News of small town events either go by unnoticed, are spread by word of mouth, or are sent to the nearest newspaper office. Upcoming events such as political meetings, a circus show, a special sale in a local store, or a community dance with a well-known musician or group are often announced in some communities by a roving motor vehicle equipped with a loudspeaker. At other times flyers are distributed house by house to announce such activities. And for diffusion of written information there is a postal system.

The Postal System

The stereotypical idea that the postal system is slow and unreliable in the Hispanic world is, in fact, true in some areas. Though mail sent out of these countries may take a couple of weeks to reach its destination, most deliveries generally average seven to ten days. It is often recommended that important documents or belongings of greater value be sent by *correo certificado* (registered mail).

As in other countries around the world, technology is providing new forms of communication for many Hispanic communities. Alternatives such as FAX and e-mail, for example, are providing services that are faster and more reliable than the postal system.

Letter-Writing Traditions

In writing letters, either personal or informal, certain guidelines are practiced by this culture. While those areas of the letter that reflect most the cultural idiosyncrasies are the sections of salutation, the introductory paragraph, and the closing, even addressing the envelope has its accepted patterns. Several of these practices are illustrated in more detail below.

The Personal Letter. At the beginning of the personal letter, the salutation sets the tone for the level of intimacy. If the letter is being sent to a family member or a very good friend, the more common salutations in the Hispanic culture are:

"Querida Carmen" or *"Querido Juan"* ("Dear Carmen" or "Dear Juan")
"Querido amigo" ("Dear Friend")
"Querida hermana" ("Dear Sister")

"Estimada amiga" ("Esteemed Friend") and *"Apreciado amigo"* ("Appreciated Friend") are often utilized in writing to acquaintances and casual friends. When a family is being addressed, the salutation should read *"Querida familia Alvarado."* On addressing a married couple where only the first names are used, the husband's name is placed first, *"Queridos Ramón y Ana."* If a touch of affection is desired, *"muy"* can be added to the salutation:

"Muy querida hermana" ("Very Dear Sister")
"Muy apreciado amigo" ("Very Appreciated Friend")
"Muy querida familia" ("Very Dear Family")

Another way to express this sentiment is to utilize the absolute superlative form of these adjectives, as is illustrated in the following:

"Queridísimo papá" ("Dearest Father")
"Apreciadísima hermana" ("Most Appreciated Sister")
"Estimadísimos amigos" ("Most Esteemed Friends")

Most personal letters begin with an introductory paragraph that is fairly formal and routine:

Querido Carlos:
    Espero que al recibir ésta te encuentres bien de salud junto a tu estimada familia. Nosotros, gracias a Dios, todos estamos bien.

Dear Carlos,
    Hopefully at the time you receive this, you and your family are feeling well. Thank God, we are all fine.

The closing of personal letters also tends to fall into a fairly formal and expected pattern. The writer traditionally sends greetings to other persons connected with the recipient of the letter, includes a sentence of farewell, and then concludes with a signature. Examples of this closing paragraph follow:

Salúdame a toda la familia. Recibe un fuerte abrazo de tu hermano que te quiere,

Miguel

Say "hello" to the whole family for me. Receive a big hug from your brother who loves you,

Miguel

Les enviamos nuestros saludos a todos. Con muchos besos y mucho cariño se despide tu hermana que te ama mucho,

Carmen

We send our greetings to all of you. With many kisses, much caring, and love, your sister says good-bye,

Carmen

Examples of other informal closings for the personal letter include:

"Con cariño" ("With love")
"Cariñosamente" ("Lovingly")
"Con mucho amor" ("With a lot of love")
"Besos" ("Kisses")
"Abrazos" ("Hugs")
"Te quiero mucho" ("I love you a lot").

The Formal Letter. Since the formal letter usually has a single purpose, its options are less varied. Here, the sections of the salutation, the introductory sentence, and the closing follow an expected format.

The salutation for the formal letter generally begins with *"Estimado(a)"* ("Respected") but varies in the manner in which the recipient is addressed.

"Estimado Sr. Pérez" or *"Estimada Sra. Pérez"*
"Estimados Srs. Montalvo"
"Estimado don Alvaro" or *"Estimada doña Jania"*
"Estimada familia Gómez"

If the addressee has a professional title, it can be included as in *"Estimado Prof. Castro"* or *"Estimada Dra. Peña."*

Most formal letters then begin with an introductory sentence that explains the object of the letter. Examples follow:

Estimado Sr. Romero:
Mucho le agradecería que me enviara el siguiente material.

Dear Mr. Romero:
I would very much appreciate your sending me the following material.

Estimada Dra. Alicea:
De acuerdo a su amable carta del 22 de octubre.

Dear Dr. Alicea:
According to your kind letter dated October 22.

Frequently concluding the formal letter is a short farewell sentence that does not end with a period but is completed, in a sense, by the phrase that follows it. The phrase utilized is usually "Sincerely," or "Attentively."

En espera de su respuesta, queda
          Sinceramente,

Waiting for your answer, I remain
          Sincerely,

An alternative to the closing is to end with a complete sentence followed by the traditional *"Cordialmente,"* ("Cordially,") or *"Sinceramente,"* ("Sincerely").

The Envelope. Whether the letter is personal or formal, the name of the *destinatario* (addressee) is written with an appropriate title. Often an abbreviated form of the title is used.

Sr. Camilo Torres	*Sra. Petronila Rosario*
Sr. Dn. Francisco Abad	*Sra. Dña. Juana Fuentes*
Prof. Juan Durán	*Dra. Idna Castellón*
Srtas. María y Teresa Robles	

If the letter is sent to an entire family, the envelope should be addressed to the person who is head of the family with *"y familia"* following the name on the same line. It is appropriate to abbreviate *"y familia"* as *"y Fam."* In addition, if a letter is sent to a husband and wife, it is addressed with the husband's name followed by *"y señora"* or *"y esposa."*

Sr. René Buendía y familia
Sra. Ana Julia Rolón y Fam.
Sr. René Buendía y señora
Sr. Dn. José Rodríguez y esposa

The name and address of the *remitente* (sender) may appear on the back of the envelope at the top center of the closed flap, or on the front top left corner of the envelope. The return address is introduced with *"Rmte.,"* which is the abbreviation for *"remitente"* or *"remite,"* a verb deriving from *"remitir,"* meaning "to send."

Rmte.   Berta Meléndez
Barrio El Campito
Barranquitas, P.R. 00609

Greeting and Announcement Cards

The tradition of sending greeting cards for special events is practiced only occasionally in this culture. Even though recently birthday and sympathy cards and invitations to weddings have become more prevalent, the personal touch of a telephone call or a visit is a more typical response to the special occasions of life. Traditionally, *la palabra* (one's spoken word) has tended to be valued more than the word that is written.

23

Education and Politics

To our surprise, my sister, who was a student in the University of Puerto Rico in the 1960s, suddenly moved home in the middle of the week. She informed us that a strike was in progress and that classes were suspended indefinitely. The reason for the strike, she explained, was to request more student participation in the university's decision-making. The conflict was further compounded by the fact that the supposed instigators were students classified as "Communists" by the institution's administration. Through media coverage, we heard a few days later that one young woman was killed while watching the action from a balcony. After several weeks of the strike, classes resumed and my sister was able to return to the university.

As a graduate student in the same university a few years later, I too experienced political interference with the educational process. This time it was evident through the political propaganda that spread in and out of the classroom. Some of my professors would at times openly express their political opinions and choices in the lecture setting. Meanwhile, many of my university friends were active proponents on campus of the independence movement, a minority political party that promoted independence for the Island. It became clear to me that although the university was an educational institution, it also served as the nucleus of activity for political issues. It thus aligned intellectualism, scholarship, and politics as uncomfortable allies in the educational experience.

THE EDUCATIONAL SYSTEM

Despite the broad geographical span, many Spanish-language countries share common characteristics in their educational systems. The following paragraphs describe each level of education in more detail.

The Elementary and Secondary Level

One shared tradition of most elementary and secondary schools, both public and private, is the use of uniforms, thus eliminating visible differences in social backgrounds. On the majority of the campuses, the boys wear slacks and shirts and the girls blouses with skirts or jumpers in colors chosen by the administration. In a few schools, a light-colored outer garment similar to a laboratory coat is the chosen uniform.

Some other common characteristics include teaching methodology, funding shortages, and educational options. The method of teaching tends to emphasize considerable memorization and recitation with less student participation. In addition, low funding in many schools has a direct impact on supplemental learning opportunities such as laboratories, libraries, audiovisual materials, and other pedagogical equipment. And as an alternative to the traditional curriculum, some schools specialize in a foreign language such as English, French, or German, and integrate that language into all of the courses.

Many communities offer both public and private school options. Very often the private institutions are operated by a church, with the Roman Catholic denomination being the most common. Parents who are financially able to do so frequently send their children to private schools. Not only is the instruction and environment considered to be of better quality, but the ability to sent one's children to a private school has status merit.

Although *la escuela primaria* (elementary school) typically includes six years, some institutions incorporate the seventh and eighth grades. Classroom size at this level in the public school often averages between thirty-five to forty students; sometimes more.

Characteristically, *la escuela secundaria* (secondary school) also consists of six years. *"La secundaria," "el colegio,"* and *"el liceo"* are other terms used to designate this educational level. If the school specifically prepares students for university studies, it is called *"la preparatoria.*" The degree of *bachiller* or *bachillerato* is earned when the high school studies and a series of government-controlled examinations are successfully completed.

Postsecondary Education

The competition for admission to public universities is very intense. Partly responsible is the fact that all government-funded universities are free or have very low tuition. Once accepted into the university, the student works towards a *título* (degree) in a very structured program with few, if any, electives. Examples of some of these *títulos* include, among others, the following:

licenciatura, a degree in the arts and sciences
arquitectura, architecture
ingeniería, engineering
maestría, master's degree
doctorado, M.D. or Ph.D.

At the university a student enrolls immediately into a single school known as a *facultad*, such as *la Facultad de Filosofía y Letras* (the humanities) or *la Facultad de Leyes o Derecho* (law), for example. Each specialization has a set of carefully prescribed courses to be taken each semester, quite distinct from the liberal arts approach found in other educational systems.

The classes are conducted in a very structured and formal manner, most generally taking the form of a lecture with little time for discussion. Classes tend to be large, ranging from fifty to several hundred students. Final grades depend on the results of one comprehensive exam, graded on a numerical scale of one to ten.

Neither sororities, fraternities, nor residence halls are common on university campuses. If the institution is a distance from home, the options for a student include staying with a relative, residing in *una pensión* (a boarding house), or renting an apartment. If the option of *una pensión* is chosen, boarders frequently share rooms as well as other facilities.

Since sports are important but never organized on a grand scale, extracurricular possibilities are limited. Students wanting to participate in a sport usually join a private club.

University professors are held in very high esteem in this culture and are frequently appointed to political and diplomatic positions. A great number of them teach part-time in addition to other employment, often teaching more for prestige than for monetary compensation. Few universities employ professors full-time.

The relationship between professor and student in the majority of the universities is formal. The professor is considered an authority who should not be doubted or questioned. In addition, the larger classes do not lend themselves to a great deal of individual student attention or discussion.

Very few universities have the privilege of a lawn-covered campus with all of the buildings in the same location or vicinity. Many universities consist of a single structure, of several buildings clustered together, or various buildings scattered throughout the city.

Besides public and private universities, there are also some junior or community colleges, more commonly known as *universidades pequeñas*. Additionally, when possible, many young adults pursue a university education abroad in places such as the United States, Canada, or Europe.

THE UNIVERSITY AND POLITICS

In general, university students are very cognizant of the social and economical problems of their country, and many are active in its politics. Campus elections frequently go beyond student issues to an attempt to influence broader political decisions. Thus, when social unrest is felt at the national level, university campuses often respond with protests, demonstrations, and even strikes. At such a time, the university may shut down for a day or even a number of weeks, raising doubts as to whether such a political atmosphere is favorable to academic learning.

POLITICS

The spirit of politics permeates many aspects of Hispanic society. In any setting, political opinions frequently enter friendly conversations, with forthright expressions on both sides of the issues. Sometimes these turn into very vigorous statements against the governmental system and its politicians. While it is acceptable for a citizen of the country to express criticism, a visitor to the culture wisely shies away from any candid expression of personal views.

The actual political campaign in many Hispanic countries is full of color, noise, and action. In the weeks prior to election day, party flags fly from cars and from the roofs of residences and businesses. Horns on vehicles tap out the code of the favored party. Traffic bogs down as long lines of pedestrians and vehicles parade down streets and roads, vigorously announcing their candidate of choice through loudspeakers. Meetings are packed with action, and even casual discussion on politics heats up at times to the point of physical push-and-shove. Indeed, the activity and color of election time creates an ambiance of "a whole country fiesta in a sea of flags."

fly from cars and from the roofs of residences and businesses. Horns on vehicles tap out the code of the favored party. Traffic bogs down as long lines of pedestrians and vehicles parade down streets and roads, vigorously announcing their candidate of choice through loudspeakers. Meetings are packed with action, and even casual discussion on politics heats up at times to the point of physical push-and-shove. Indeed, the activity and color of election time creates an ambiance of "a whole country fiesta in a sea of flags."

24

Measurements and Divisions of Time and Space

Built on a verdant slope in the central part of my native Caribbean island, the private elementary school I attended provided students with plenty of space for outdoor activities, fresh mountain air, and a mono-seasonal ambiance. Certainly, there was the hurricane season and the rainy season and the time of year when the grass on our slope turned a bit dry. But day in and day out the Fahrenheit thermometer registered in the seventies; our days were comfortable and life was good.

Understandably, it came as a surprise to my Spanish-speaking classmates and me when our English teacher informed us one day that in other parts of the world there were four seasons. In Ohio where she came from, she explained, each season has its own distinctive characteristics. She showed us pictures of trees losing their leaves, and of children wearing coats, caps, and mittens, and playing in the snow. Then she led us on the arduous task of memorizing and identifying these foreign-sounding words: "Spring," "Summer," "Fall," "Winter." The information seemed meaningless to me and very much out of context. I was glad when the class was over.

Years later, now living in northern Indiana, I know these four seasons well. The mercury in the Fahrenheit thermometer is constantly on the move; each day is a surprise but life is still good.

THE CLIMATE

In an area as vast as the Hispanic world, there is great diversity of climate. Essentially, three main zones are involved, spread out over the entire area: the subtropics; a hot, dry region; and a cold, mountainous area. Large desert-like areas, for example, are found not only in northern Argentina, Chile, and Mexico, but also in the highlands of Peru and Bolivia, and in central Spain. Even within a single country, the contrasts can be spectacular.

Regions in the areas south of the equator follow a reverse pattern from those in the north. That means that the coldest months in the countries located north of the equator are the warmest times in countries such as Argentina, Chile, Uruguay, and Paraguay. Also, areas near the equator typically have only two seasons of about six months each one: *la estación de las lluvias* (the rainy season) and *la estación seca* (the dry season). Costa Rica, Mexico, and Venezuela are illustrations of this pattern with warm rainy weather from about April to October, and dry, cooler days during the remainder of the year.

THE TEMPERATURE

In the majority of the Hispanic countries, the centigrade system is utilized to indicate temperatures. For those individuals who are more familiar with the Fahrenheit measurement, there is a handy formula for conversion between the two systems. To convert from centigrade to Fahrenheit, multiply the centigrade degrees by 1.8, and then add 32. Conversely, to convert from Fahrenheit to centigrade, subtract 32 from the Fahrenheit degrees, and divide the remainder by 1.8.

The following chart compares some Fahrenheit temperatures with their centigrade equivalents:

Fahrenheit:	$16°$	$32°$	$50°$	$81°$	$102°$
Centigrade:	$-9°$	$0°$	$10°$	$27°$	$39°$

In speaking about the temperature conditions, the sentence structure of *"Está a veinte y siete grados"* ("It is 27 degrees") is used. The formula is *"Está a"* + the number + the degrees. Then if the temperature drops nine degrees below zero, it is expressed as *"Está a nueve bajo cero."*

THE DATE

In the Hispanic world, *el lunes* (Monday) is considered the first day of the week and *el domingo* (Sunday) is the seventh. A week is viewed as eight days, and two weeks as fifteen since both the beginning and ending days are included. Thus a one-week activity is *una actividad de ocho días*, and activities occurring two weeks from the present will take place *de hoy en quince días*.

In addition, when the full date is written, the number of the day is indicated first, followed by the month, and then the year. For example, March 15, 1996 is written as *"15 de marzo de 1996."* A comma is sometimes placed after the month, thus eliminating the need for the preposition *"de"* between the month and year: *15 de marzo, 1996.* If the date is expressed in numerals, it appears as either *15/III/96* or *15/3/96*.

The article *"el"* is utilized when the date is part of a complete sentence as in *"Hoy es el 15 de marzo de 1996."* ("Today is March 15, 1996."). The article is not used in dating a document such as a letter or research paper: *"15 de marzo de 1996."*

Contrary to the capitalization rules in English, the days of the week and the months of the year are not capitalized.

THE TWENTY-FOUR HOUR SYSTEM

Though the twelve-hour system is used in the regular day-to-day events to measure time in Hispanic countries, the twenty-four-hour method is often utilized for official purposes. Transportation schedules and radio and television programs are the main users of this system, known as "military time." Thus, a man planning to take a plane will notify his family and friends that he is leaving *a las ocho de la noche* while his printed airline schedule will list his departure at *a las veinte horas* or *20 h.*

The twenty-four-hour system is figured by counting the hours consecutively beginning at midnight. A comparison follows:

Twenty-Four-Hour System		Twelve-Hour System
8:30 or *ocho y media*	=	*8:30 a.m.* or *las ocho y media de la mañana*
14:00 or *catorce*	=	*2:00 p.m.* or *las dos de la tarde*
22:00 or *veinte y dos*	=	*10:00 p.m.* or *las diez de la noche*

HEIGHT, WEIGHT, AND DISTANCE

Here, as in most other parts of the world, the metric system is used to measure height, weight, and distance. *Metros* define height, *kilos* describe weight, and *kilómetros* measure distance.

Height

In measuring height, one *metro* (meter) is equivalent to 3.281 feet or 39.37 inches. Figuring the reverse, 0.305 meter equals one foot and 2.54 centimeters equals one inch. To convert the height of an object measured in feet and inches into meters and centimeters, first figure in inches, then multiply by 2.54, and finally divide by 100.

To illustrate this, a person who is 5'6" or 66" is 168 centimeters tall when the 66" is multiplied by 2.54. Then, because there are 100 centimeters in a meter, the 168 centimeter measurement is divided by 100 and becomes *1 metro and 68 centimetros*.

To reverse the process and convert a measurement from meters and centimeters into feet and inches, divide the height in centimeters by 2.54.

Weight

Kilos is the measurement utilized in the metric system for weight. One kilogram is the equivalent of about 2.2 pounds, and one pound equals 454 grams. The procedure used to convert pounds to *kilos* involves dividing the weight in pounds by 2.2. Conversely, to convert *kilos* to pounds, multiply the weight in *kilos* by 2.2. Thus, a person weighing 189 pounds weighs 85.9 kilograms.

Distance

Los kilómetros measure distance. A handy formula for converting kilometers into miles is to divide the total number of kilometers by eight, and then multiply that result by five. For example, 200 kilometers divided by 8 is 25. Multiplying the 25 by 5 results in 125 miles. Thus, 200 *kilómetros* is equal to 125 *millas*.

25

The Spanish Language

We had explained to our maid in Costa Rica that even though I was from Puerto Rico, my spouse from Iowa, and our two sons from Indiana, we wanted her to cook typical food from the country as much as possible. Her almost-shy smile communicated her approval of the idea of introducing us to the enjoyment of *Tico* cuisine.

The next morning Flor informed us that for lunch we would be having a beef and vegetable soup eaten with rice. Since we had agreed to buy any needed ingredients, she handed us the list and we drove to the *Supermercado Periférico*, located close to our home.

We headed back to the vegetable section in the store, looked carefully at the list and discovered we recognized very few of the items written down. *"Con permiso,"* we said to an employee stacking eggs, "where can we find *tiquisque?*" The young man led us to an area of root vegetables and pointed to a pile of produce that in Puerto Rico we called *"yautía."* Surprised, we selected a few and moved on to the next item on the list: *"Camote."* We looked at each other and then retraced our steps to the helpful store employee. We followed him back to the same area; this time he pointed out sweet potatoes. "Interesting," I thought to myself, "my mother buys these but calls them *batatas.*" It was the same thing with sweet corn which was *"elote"* in the *Supermercado Periférico*, but *"maíz fresco"* on my island. We continued down the list, enriching our vocabulary and discovering vegetables mutually enjoyed by two Spanish-language countries. With our mission completed we drove back home, and a couple of hours later, sat down to a steaming and fragrant dish of *olla de carne*— incredibly similar to *sancocho* back home!

ORIGINS

The Spanish language has its roots in Latin. Brought to Spain by the Romans around 200 B.C., Latin later combined with other languages to provide the foundation for the Spanish of today. Because of this origin, Spanish belongs to a family of languages called the Romance languages, a grouping that also includes Italian, French, Romanian, and Portuguese. Generally known as *castellano*, the language became more commonly identified as *español* when *España* (Spain) began its colonization of the New World.

Approximately sixty percent of currently used words in Spanish can be traced directly to Latin. The remaining forty have originated from a variety of other languages that include Arabic, Greek, and Basque. Indian and African languages have contributed as well, beginning at the end of the fifteenth century with the arrival of the Spaniards to the Americas. Quechua, from the Southern Andean region; Maya, from Mexico and Guatemala; and Nahuatl, from Mexico, were some of the main Indian languages enhancing the language.

The Arabic Influence

A closer look at the Arabic influence illustrates the manner in which one of these contributors has enriched the Spanish language known today. The Muslims, who spoke Arabic, invaded the Iberian Peninsula in 711 A.D. and occupied that area until their defeat in 1492. During this span of approximately eight centuries, many Arabic words entered the Spanish language. It is said that today there are some 4,000 words of this origin in modern Spanish.

Many Spanish words that begin with "al" have their beginnings from the Arabic language: *alcohol, álgebra, alfalfa, alcoba* (bedroom), *algodón* (cotton), *almohada* (pillow). Some words beginning with "a" are also traced to Arabic: *aceite* (oil), *ajedrez* (chess), *arroz* (rice), *azúcar* (sugar), *aduana* (customs). In addition, the very common and often expressed phrase *"ojalá que"* ("I hope that") has evolved from the Arabic "May Allah grant that."

English Contributions

The English language has also contributed to Spanish vocabulary, but more recently than many of the others. This influence is most easily seen in some of the almost direct word adoptions from the English to the Spanish. Examples include words such as *suéter, jeans, jonrón* (home run), *gol, fútbol, béisbol, basquetbol, volibol, bistec*, and *sándwich.* *"El estrés"* ("stress") and *"formatear"* ("to format") are recent additions to the Spanish vocabulary. Words borrowed from the English language are usually absorbed into Spanish in the masculine gender, and although they may have varying pronunciations, they can be easily understood by an English speaker.

Reciprocally, English vocabulary has also borrowed from the Spanish language. Examples include: *aficionado, barrio, patio, taco, siesta, rodeo, sierra, vista, plaza, canal, gusto, número uno, scenario.* Names, as well, have joined the English selections, illustrated by names such as *Antonio, Anita, Maria, Carlos, Fernando, Bonita* (meaning "pretty" in Spanish), and *Dolores* (meaning "pain").

Within the United States, well-known geographical places such as *California, Nevada, Montana, Colorado, Texas, El Paso, San Francisco, Los Angeles*, and *San Diego* show the historical interactions of cultures. And even smaller towns, scattered across the United States, have borrowed from the Spanish language: *La Plata, Peru, El Dorado, Cuero,* and *Gonzales*, among others.

CURRENT USAGE

Today Spanish is the native language of over 360 million people. It is the official language of Spain; every Central American nation except Belize; all South American countries except Brazil and the Guianas; Mexico, Puerto Rico, Cuba, and the Dominican Republic. Spanish is also the first language of an estimated 25 million people living in the United States. In addition, it is the first language of hundreds of thousands of people of Hispanic background residing in Europe, the Caribbean, the Philippines, Guam, Equatorial Guinea, and northern Morocco.

Besides its function as a first language, Spanish is also a very much utilized supplement to other native languages. Millions of individuals are learning it through instruction; currently Spanish is the most popular foreign language among North American students. According to the Modern Language Association of America (MLAM), more than half of foreign language students in the United States are enrolled in Spanish courses. And although the majority of people in the Hispanic countries utilize Spanish as their first language, there are areas populated by Indians who speak their own dialect in addition to the country's official language. *Quechua*, for example, is spoken by the Indian population in Peru, Ecuador, and Bolivia; *Náhuatl* is used in Mexico; and *Guaraní* in Paraguay. There are also other clusters in this region, such as in the jungles of the Amazon or in the Andes, that are populated by indigenous tribes who speak only native languages.

Regional Variations

Because language is alive and constantly changing with the life and adaptations of an area, names for food and objects, verbal expressions, and even pronunciations and accents will understandably vary. Such is the reality with the Spanish language. As described in the vignette at the beginning of this chapter, the names of vegetables, fruits, and food in general are especially noted for their variation from area to area. Objects of Indian or African background also are recognized by distinct names depending on the region.

Terminology used in the area of transportation is very illustrative of this diversity of vocabulary. For example, the word "automobile" is generally known as *un automóvil*, but is also called *un carro* in Puerto Rico and Colombia, *un coche* in Spain, and *un auto* in Argentina. Meanwhile the term for "bus," which is often called *autobús*, is also known as *una guagua* in Puerto Rico and Cuba, *un camión* in Mexico, *un bus* in Colombia and Costa Rica, and *un ómnibus* in Argentina. At times these variations lead to confusion since *un camión* is also a truck in the greater part of the Spanish-language world, while *una guagua* refers to a small baby in Chile and Bolivia. Generally, though, the context in which the word is used or a quick question clarifies any confusion created by vocabulary differences.

Besides word usage, regional variations are also observable in the use of certain verbal expressions. *"¡Pura vida!"* ("Great!") and *"chunches"* ("things"), for example, would hint of a Costa Rican connection. *"¡Nítido!"* or *"¡Chévere!"* (Puerto Rico), *"¡Un fenómeno!"* or *"¡De película!"* (Cuba), *"¡Macanudo!"* (Argentina), *"¡Padre!"* (Mexico) are all phrases that show excitement, approval and interest—as well as nationality.

Going beyond the use of words or phrases, certain speech characteristic also tend to define regional influences. These include the dropping of word endings, the distinct pronunciation of specific consonants, and lilting tonality patterns. It is through peculiarities such as these that a speaker could be identified as coming from Puerto Rico, Mexico, Argentina, Spain, or other particular area of Hispanic America.

The Use of Diminutives

Diminutive suffixes are used frequently in current Spanish, with the most common endings being *"-ito"* or *"-cito."* One of the main uses of the diminutive is to describe a smaller size: *una casita* (a small house) or *un puentecito* (a small bridge). But there are other functions of the diminutive as well. The suffixes can be used to show affection as with *"mi hermanita,"* even if the sister is 6'1" tall and is forty-five years old. Use of the diminutive can indicate rejection such as to describe someone as *feíto* (ugly). It can soften the impact of a request: *"¿Puede hacerme un prestamito?"* ("Would you be able to give me a loan?"); tone down a command: *"¡Despacito, despacito!"* ("Slow down, slow down!"); or make it easier to verbalize a delicate issue: *"El está muy enfermito."* ("He is very, very ill.").

Proverbs and Sayings

The Spanish language is rich in *proverbios* (proverbs) and *dichos* or *refranes* (sayings) that are frequently sprinkled into informal and everyday conversation. Originating in both oral and written tradition, they provide a touch of humor and color to colloquial language. It is essential to know the context in which a proverb or saying is used in order to understand it adequately.

The ideas contained in some proverbs and sayings are quite similar in Spanish and English even though the phrases that have evolved may be unique. Several examples that show these similarities follow:

1. *Más vale tarde que nunca.*
   Better late than never.
2. *A quien madruga, Dios le ayuda.* (God helps those who arise early.)
   The early bird catches the first worm.
3. *Las paredes oyen.*
   The walls have ears.
4. *No se ganó Zamora en una noche.* (Zamora was not won in one night.)
   Rome wasn't built in a day.
5. *Está entre la espada y la pared.* (S/he is between the sword and the wall.)
   S/he is between a rock and a hard place.

6. *Más vale pájaro en mano que cien volando.* (Of more worth is a bird in the hand than one hundred flying.)
   A bird in hand is worth more than two in a bush.
7. *Más sabe el diablo por viejo que por diablo.* (The devil knows more from being old than for being himself.)
   With age comes wisdom.
8. *Habla hasta por los codos.* (S/he talks too much, overflows at the elbows.)
   Habla más que una vieja sin tabaco. (S/he talks more than an old woman without tobacco.)
   "S/he runs off at the mouth."
   "S/he talks till s/he is blue in the face."
9. *De tal palo, tal astilla.* (As the tree, so the splinter.)
   A chip off the old block.
10. *Ojo por ojo; diente por diente.*
    An eye for an eye; a tooth for a tooth.

While *dichos* or *refranes* through frequent use can assist in defining and expressing culture, they can also reflect past cultural influences. The Caribbean saying, *"El que no tiene dinga tiene mandinga"* ("If it's not one thing, it's another"), illustrates this. In its use of *"dinga"* and *"mandinga"* it borrows from its African roots.

26

Ethnic Diversity and Contribution

He left his native land in southern Spain and boarded an old dilapidated ship to cross an unknown ocean. Weeks later he stepped onto the shores of Argentina in search of adventure and improved economic well-being. As passing months took their toll on the young man's dream, he again left on a ship, this time with the destination of the Caribbean island of Puerto Rico. There he found work on a farm in the mountainous interior of the island, and with conscientious work and astute decisions soon became owner of his own *finca*. In time he married a native islander, an attractive young woman with a skin color not as white as his own.

Today the descendants of this Spaniard and his Caribbean spouse are known by the name of *"Falcón."* And, like most other Island residents, they are a mosaic of skin color and hair characteristics, enhanced through decades of marriage choices from Puerto Rico's dominant ethnic sources: Spanish, African, and Caribbean Indian. My father, a third-generation descendent of the young man from Spain, is illustrative of this. A sun-tanned man of average height with blue eyes and straight black hair, he married my mother who was short of stature and whose light skin color, tiny facial features, and very thick black hair were genetic evidence of her racial wealth: White, Black and Indian.

My siblings and I are now the fourth generation and serve as a microcosm of the physical diversity experienced by the broader Hispanic world. We are of average height, taller and shorter. We have blue eyes, green eyes, and brown eyes. Our hair is straight, curly, black, dark brown, thick, and silky. Our skin color is white to dark sun-tanned. Yet, we all share the same heritage, speak the same language, and live as a family, proud of the beauty our racial and ethnic background has given us.

ETHNIC AND RACIAL BACKGROUNDS

Due to the size of its population and its wide geographical distribution, the Hispanic world experiences great ethnic diversity alongside its common language. Illustrating this are the populations of Mexico and South and Central America who are mainly of Indian, European, and *mestizo* (a mixture of Indian and European races) background; the peoples of the Caribbean whose ethnic roots are Indian, European, and African; or those in Spain with the physical characteristics of Celts, Romans, and Arabs who conquered and colonized the Iberian Peninsula.

So even though dark eyes, black hair, and olive complexion are often considered characteristics of a person with Hispanic roots, millions who live in this area do not fit the stereotype. There are Spanish Americans, for example, coming from areas of significant European influence, as in Argentina, Uruguay or northern Spain. Challenging the stereotype also are the native Spanish speakers of African, Asian, or Middle Eastern descent who have been residents of Hispanic countries for several generations. Many of them emigrated years ago in search of opportunities for a better life, and today enjoy a prosperous and successful life as active and productive members of the Hispanic world.

This ethnic and racial diversity has the potential of bringing a rich presence to homogeneous communities. It is in these settings that stories and legends from the past can be shared, that meals and recipes can be swapped, that children speaking distinct native languages in their homes can play together in a neighborhood playground, and that commonalities can be discovered. Each person contributes to the wealth of that community, whether newly arrived, a second-generation resident, or a member of a family with a long history in the area.

THE HISPANIC PRESENCE IN THE UNITED STATES

A classic example of this wealth, interconnection, and ethnic contribution is the Hispanic presence in the United States. Most Hispanics are not recent immigrants to the country. For many, residency can be traced back to the nineteenth century and even earlier, when family members lived in the Mexican territory, which today is the southwestern United States. Whether native to the area or immigrant, one tenth of the population (more than 22 million people) in the United States today identify themselves as Hispanic. In terms of the number of residents of Hispanic origin, the United States ranks fifth in the world following Mexico, Spain, Colombia, and Argentina, in that order. And although there is representation from all the Hispanic countries residing in the United States, three groups are predominant. The largest group (60%) are Mexicans, who are located primarily in California, Texas, and the southwestern part of the country. The second group are the Puerto Ricans (14%), who are found largely in New York City, Chicago, and other urban centers of the Northeast. The third group are the Cubans (6%), mainly living in southern Florida. The remaining 20% is composed of individuals from the other countries, but primarily from Colombia, the Dominican Republic, and El Salvador.

Their ethnic presence and contribution to life in the United States can be especially noted through storytelling and legends of the country's past. Spanish explorers and Mexican settlers left their mark throughout the country from Florida to California. *San Agustín* or Saint Augustine, for example, is one of the oldest cities in the country, having been founded in 1565 by a Spaniard, Pedro Menéndez de Avilés. Many history books detail the route of the Spanish explorers through territory that today is the United States.

In addition, as has been noted throughout this book, there has also been an interconnectedness and ethnic contribution in the areas of food, music, sports, entertainment and vocabulary. This ongoing cultural borrowing, adapting, loss and enrichment is an essential part of daily life experience where members of ethnic groups live together in integrated communities around the world, passing on their wealth from one generation to the next.

Conclusions

The Hispanic culture is a rich conglomeration created through years of history and generations of people, each adding their particular essence to the whole. Each contribution added to another has achieved a synergetic wealth that transcends the value of the single part.

Even though the richness of the Hispanic culture can be attributed to many factors, some, in my opinion, are more essential than others. Hispanics are people of the heart, and people of honor, dignity, respect, and defined beliefs. This has created an energetic, emotive, gesticulating, and life-filled culture, distinct from any other on the planet earth.

The presence of the Catholic Church has provided a intrinsic background for many of the traditions that today are accepted as a natural and integral part of the culture. The social support of the *"compadrazgo"* system and celebrations such as Christmas, Holy Week, and the Festival of the Patron Saint are examples of this.

Climate and weather have helped to create additional cultural characteristics. The *guayabera* shirt, *la plaza*, *la siesta*, and home remedies derived from plants are but a few examples.

The open display of affection, the warmth of hospitality, the importance of respect in attitude and speech, and the actions of formality are patterns integral to this culture.

No culture is static; it continues to change and be changed. The Hispanic culture illustrates this reality. The technological advances that bombard modern society, the many Hispanics returning to their homeland after having lived abroad, the foreigners from diverse ethnic backgrounds establishing themselves in Hispanic territory are just a few of the agents responsible for the transculturation process.

"Salsa" as rhythm and music expresses creatively the essence of Hispanic culture. Just as it combines various musical elements to create candescence, color, and spirit, so the Hispanic culture mixes together a variety of essential ingredients to fashion an active, energetic, and beautiful entity.

Equally, *"salsa"* as a culinary sauce takes a variety of spices and vegetables and in their combination creates a plate that is attractive, tasty, and unique. For me, Hispanic culture is a lot like *"salsa."* Everything is altogether in one dish with a lot of *"sabor."* Very essential to its character is each ingredient, individually unique, yet complementary.

Glossary

a crédito.   On credit
abuela, la.   Grandmother
"Adiós, guapa (linda, mamacita)."   "Bye, Cutie"
ajonjolí, el.   Sesame seed candy
"A las órdenes."   "At your service"
arroz con dulce, el.   Sweet rice
"así así."   "So-so"

bacalao con huevos, el.   Codfish with eggs
banderilleros, los.   The bullfighter who uses colorful sticks called *banderillas*
barrio, el.   Neighborhood
batatas, las.   Sweet potatoes
bendición, la.   The blessing
besos, los.   Kisses

café con leche, el.   Coffee with milk
café, el.   Coffee
cafecito, el.   Coffee; used interchangeably with *el café*
camarero, el.   Waiter
camote, el.   Sweet potato
campo, el.   Countryside
ciego, el.   A blind person (male)
"Claro, hijo."   "Of course, Son"
clínica, la.   Clinic
coco, el.   Coconut
cojo, el.   A person who limps (male)
compadres, los.   Good friends or companions

corrida de toros, la.   Bullfight
cuenta, la.   The bill

delicias, las.   Delights
deseo.   I want
día del maestro, el.   Teachers' Day
día del santo, el.   Saint's Day
"Dios te bendiga."   "God bless you"
disculpe.   Excuse; forgive
doctora, la.   Female doctor
dulce de coco, el.   Coconut candy

elote.   Sweet corn
"Encantado (de conocerlo/a)."   "I am delighted to meet you"
"Entren, ésta es su casa."   "Enter, this is your home"
"Es un placer conocerlo/a."   "It is a pleasure to meet you"

favor, el.   A favor
feo, el.   An ugly person (male)
fiesta, la.   A party
fiestas patronales, las.   Celebrations in honor of a patron saint
finca, la.   A farm
flaquito, el.   A skinny person (male)
fotonovelas, las.   A soap opera communicated through written publications
         with photos

gordito, el.   A chubby person (male)
guapa.   Refers to a pretty woman or girl; frequently utilized in catcalls
guayabas, las.   Guavas
güiro, el.   A pre-Columbian instrument that remains in use in folk, popular
         and commercial Latin American music, especially in the Caribbean.
         The instrument is made from a gourd with parallel grooves cut
         horizontally on one side. A wooden brush with wire bristles
         scraping over the grooves produces its rhythmic contribution

hacer.   To do or make
hospital, el.   Hospital

ingeniero, el.   Engineer
íntimo.   Intimate

kiosko, el.   Kiosk

lechón asado, el.   Roast pig
licenciado, el.   A bachelor's degree; a lawyer (male)
limosna, la.   Alms

madrina, la. Godmother

maestra, la. Teacher (female)

mamey, un. "Peaches 'n cream"

mampostiales, los. Candy from a mixture of coconut and molasses

mañana. Tomorrow

"más o menos." "More or less"

"¿Me cuidas?" "Will you take care of me?"

medio luto. "Medium" mourning

mesero, el. Waiter

mestizo, el. A person of European and Indian descent

mozo, el. Waiter

"Mucho gusto en conocerlo/a." "It brings me pleasure to meet you"

muda, la. A mute person (female)

nieto, el. Grandson

novios, los. May refer to a boyfriend and girlfriend; an engaged couple

padrino, el. Godfather

pan caliente, el. Hot bread

pan de manteca, el. A bread with an appearance similar to French bread that uses lard or vegetable shortening

pan de agua, el. A bread with an appearance similar to French bread that uses a generous amount of water as its liquid ingredient

pan fresquito, el. Fresh bread

pan, el. Bread

panadería, la. Bakery; bread shop

"Para servirle." "I am here to serve you"

parrandas, las. Hispanic Christmas tradition similar to Christmas caroling in the United States

pasteles, los. In appearance this dish is similar to the Mexican tamale, with the exception that small chunks of pork or chicken are rolled in a mixture of root vegetables, green bananas and plantains. It is then wrapped in banana leaves, tied with string, and cooked in boiling water

pedir la entrada a la casa. To request visiting privileges

perdón. Pardon

piña, la. Pineapple

piragüero, el. A vendor of snow cones

piropos, los. Catcalls

plaza, la. Plaza; town square

ponche, el. Eggnog

profesora, la. Professor (female)

"pues, ahí." "Well, there"

prieto. Black

pumagasas, las. A pear-like fruit that has a red exterior when ripe

queso de bola holandés, el.   Gouda cheese; a mild cheese in the shape of a flat
                                sphere, often coated with red wax, and named
                                after Gouda, Holland, its place of origin
"¿Quieres ser mi novia?"   "Do you want to be my girlfriend?"
quiero.   I want
quinceañero, el.   The fifteenth birthday party which celebrates a girl's pas-
                     sage from childhood to womanhood
"Quisiera presentarle a ..."   "I would like to introduce you to ..."

radionovelas, las.   A soap opera performed over the radio
roble, el.   Oak tree
rompope, el.   Eggnog

sabor, el.   Taste; flavor
Semana Santa.   Holy Week
señal de la cruz, la.   The sign of the cross
señor, el.   Man
señora, la.   Lady
señorita, la.   Young lady
servidor, un.   Your servant
sorda, la.   A deaf person (female)

tamales, los.   A typical food with chopped fried meat rolled in a cornmeal
                  dough, wrapped in corn husks or banana leaves, and then
                  steamed
tamarindo, el.   Tamarind
"Tanto gusto."   "Pleased to meet you"
"Te presento a."   "I introduce you to"
tienda, la.   A store
tiquisque, el.   An edible root
torero, el.   Bullfighter
tranquila.   More peaceful
turista, el/la.   Tourist

visita, la.   An informal and spontaneous visit to the homes of friends, neigh-
                bors, or family

yautía.   An edible root

Bibliography

Béjar Navarro, Raúl. *El mexicano, aspectos culturales y psico-sociales.* México: Universidad Nacional Autónoma de México, 1981.

Biesanz, Richard, Karen Zubris Biesanz and Mavis Hiltunen Biesanz. *The Costa Ricans.* Englewood Cliffs, New Jersey: Prentice-Hall, Inc., 1982.

Braganti, N.L. and E. Devine. *The Traveler's Guide to Latin American Customs and Manners.* New York: St. Martin's Press, 1988.

Cantarino, Vicente. *Civilización y cultura de España.* New York: MacMillan Publishing Company, 1988.

Cirre, José F. and Manuela M. Cirre. *España y los españoles.* New York: Holt, Rinehart and Winston, Inc., 1981.

Copeland, John G., Ralph Kite and Lynn Sandstedt. *Cultura y civilización.* New York: Holt, Rinehart and Winston, Inc., 1989.

Cordasco, Francesco and Eugene Bucchioni. *The Puerto Rican Experience: A Sociological Source Book.* Totowa, New Jersey: Little Field, Adams and Company, 1973.

Crescioni Neggers, Gladys. *Breve introducción a la cultura puertorriqueña.* Madrid: Editorial Playor, S.A., 1986.

Díaz Plaja, Fernando. *El español y los siete pecados capitales.* Madrid: Alianza Editorial, 1975.

Gann, L.H. and Peter J. Duignan. *The Hispanics in the United States.* Boulder, Colorado: Westview Press, 1986.

Gómez Tabanera, José Manuel, ed. *El foklore español.* Madrid: Instituto Español de Antropología Aplicada, 1968.

Hendricks, Glenn. *The Dominican Diaspora: From the Dominican Republic to New York City—Villagers in Transition.* New York: Teachers College Press, 1974.

168 Bibliography

Henríquez Ureña, Pedro. *Historia de la cultura en la América Hispánica.* México: Fondo de Cultura Económica, 1947.

Hilton, Ronald. *The Latin Americans. Their Heritage and Their Destiny.* New York: J.B. Lippincott Company, 1973.

Hinds, Harold E. and Charles M. Tatum, eds. *Handbook of Latin American Popular Culture.* Westport, Connecticut: Greenwood Press, 1985.

Introduction to the Latin American Nations. Washington, DC: The Department of Information and Public Affairs, Organization of American States, 1970.

Kattan Ibarra, Juan. *Perspectivas culturales de Hispanoamérica.* Lincolnwood, Illinois: National Textbook Company, 1989.

Kohls, L. Robert. *Developing Intercultural Awareness.* Washington, DC: SIETAR, 1981.

Lewald, Ernest H. *Latinoamérica: sus culturas y sociedades.* New York: McGraw-Hill, Inc., 1973.

Ludwig, Ed and James Santibáñez, eds. *The Chicanos. Mexican American Voices.* Baltimore, Maryland: Penguin Books, Inc., 1973.

Marger, Martin N. *Race and Ethnic Relations.* Belmont, California: Wadsworth Publishing Company, 1985.

Michener, James A. *Iberia: Spanish Travels and Reflections.* New York: Random House, 1968.

Moncada, Alberto. *Norteamérica con acento hispánico.* Madrid: Instituto de Cooperación Iberoamericana, 1988.

Moore, Joan and Harry Pachon. *Hispanics in the United States.* Englewood Cliffs, New Jersey: Prentice-Hall, Inc., 1985.

Nine Curt, Carmen Judith. *Non-verbal Communication.* Cambridge, Massachusetts: National Assessment and Dissemination Center for Bilingual/Bicultural Education, 1976.

Picón Salas, Mariano. *De la conquista a la independencia. Tres siglos de historia cultural hispanoamericana.* México: Fondo de Cultura Económica, 1950.

Pritchett, V.S. *The Spanish Temper.* New York: Harper and Row Publishers, 1965.

Prohías, Rafael J. and Lourdes Casal. *The Cuban Minority in the U.S.* Boca Raton, Florida: Cuban Minority Planning Study, Florida Atlantic University, 1973.

Sardiña, Ricardo R. *Breve historia de Hispanoamérica.* Cincinnati, Ohio: Southwestern Publishing Company, 1982.

Stevens, Evelyn P. "Marianismo, The Other Face of Machismo in Latin America," in Ann Pascatello, ed., *Female and Male in Latin America.* Pittsburgh: University of Pittsburgh Press, 1973.

Urbanski, Edmun Stephen. *Hispanic America and its Civilizations.* Oklahoma City: University of Oklahoma Press, 1978.

Vogel Zanger, Virginia. *Exploración intercultural. Una guía para el estudiante.* Massachusetts: Newbury House Publishers, Inc., 1984.

Index

About the Author and Collaborator

RAFAEL FALCÓN is Professor of Spanish in the Foreign Language Department at Goshen College, Goshen, Indiana.

CHRISTINE YODER FALCÓN is Director of the Learning Resources Center at Goshen College.

ISBN 0-275-96121-4

90000>

HARDCOVER BAR CODE